THE HEYDAY OF
SIR WALTER SCOTT

By the same Author

ARTICULATE ENERGY
An Inquiry into the Syntax of
English Poetry

A WINTER TALENT
and other poems

THE HEYDAY OF
SIR WALTER
SCOTT

by

DONALD DAVIE

Fellow of Gonville and Caius College
Cambridge

Barnes & Noble, Inc.

NEW YORK

First published in U.S.A. 1961
by Barnes & Noble, Inc.
New York

© Donald Davie 1961

Printed in Great Britain

CONTENTS

INTRODUCTION

At bottom this is no more than a report on desultory reading over several years, mostly in books that were once more fashionable than they are now. I have enjoyed this reading, I try to explain why, and I pass on the tips for what they are worth.

However, because all of these works by common consent hang together, being all products of the one well-defined phase of literary history which my title indicates, I have not been able to consider them together without raising certain larger issues: what romanticism is, and what its enduring value is—at least as it expresses itself in the novel; what 'plot' means, and how important it is, in the novel; and what 'realism' means.

I believe it is true that Scott is nowadays read more often by people for whom literature is a marginal interest than by those for whom it is central; more often by scientists, for instance, than by professional students of literature. I think this is a great pity. And in the course of this book I try to say why.

I

THE CAPTAIN'S DAUGHTER: PUSHKIN'S PROSE AND RUSSIAN REALISM

P USHKIN'S historical novel *The Captain's Daughter* is a story of the experiences of Pyotr Andreyitch Grinyov, son of a Russian country gentleman, inheriting a tradition of martial and loyalist service, in the period of the Cossack rebellion of Pugatchov in the seventeen-seventies. Grinyov, travelling to his first garrison, is helped by an anonymous Cossack to whom he makes in return a small gift. After an interview in Orenburg with his general, he is appointed to a small garrison in territory still not entirely conquered from the Bashkirs and Kirghiz. The commander of the garrison, Captain Mironov, is a simple old soldier, much under the thumb of his admirable and upright wife, and has a paternal attitude to the troops under his command. Grinyov gradually falls in love with the captain's daughter, and fights a duel on her behalf with the other junior officer, Shvabrin, an exiled rake. Grinyov is wounded, but recovers in time to see Pugatchov and the rebel Cossacks take the 'fortress'. Shvabrin turns traitor and the Mironovs are brutally executed, but Pugatchov, revealed as the anonymous Cossack of the earlier incident, allows Grinyov to escape, to help in the defence of Orenburg

I

against the rebels. The captain's daughter, however, Marya Ivanovna, is left in the hands of Shvabrin, and Grinyov again enlists the aid of Pugatchov to release her. He rejoins the loyalist forces and is able to defend the paternal estate against the rebels under Shvabrin, but when the rising is finally quelled, he faces a court-martial because of his dealings with Pugatchov. He is saved by the personal intervention of the Empress, after Marya Ivanovna has enlisted her aid.

When Pushkin's English translator remarks[1], with reference to *The Captain's Daughter*:

> The realism so characteristic of Pushkin's writing is the keynote of Russian literature as a whole,

no reader, I suppose, will account himself materially assisted. It is arguable that the novel is necessarily more realistic than other forms, as incapable of a high degree of abstraction; any category which includes, by implication, both Tolstoy and Dostoievsky, cannot easily mean anything more specific. Russian literature is richer in good novels than in good poems; that, it seems, is all that is implied in talk of 'Russian realism'. Still, Pushkin's influence was, when all due respect has been paid to Gogol and to Western Romantics, so considerable, that to examine what meaning can be allowed to 'realism' in relation to Pushkin's prose is likely to enlighten also an understanding of later Russian fiction.

The coarsest gloss on 'realism' will represent it as a photographic fidelity to appearance. And this, at any rate, cannot stand as just with reference to *The Captain's Daughter*:

> 'Well, lads', the Commandant said, 'now open the gates, beat the drum. Forward, children; come out, follow me!'
> The Commandant, Ivan Ignatyitch, and I were instantly beyond the rampart; but the garrison lost their nerve and did not move.

---

[1] Natalie Duddington, Introduction to Everyman edition.

'Why do you stand still, children?' Ivan Kuzmitch shouted. 'If we must die, we must—it's all in the day's work!'

At that moment the rebels ran up to us and rushed into the fortress. The drum stopped; the soldiers threw down their rifles; I was knocked down, but got up again and walked into the fortress together with the rebels.

The representation of action is here as stylized as the treatment of the direct speech. Very obviously, no attempt is made to render faithfully the sense of the hurly-burly, to bring before the mind's eye anything but a selective picture. 'The Commandant, Ivan Ignatyitch, and I were instantly beyond the rampart . . .' The effect is as unnatural as the rapidity and conclusiveness of movement in the early films. Movement, in fact, is not presented at all; only a sequence of tableaux. Of course, this method is a characteristic of the period. One finds it for instance in *The Last of the Mohicans* when the heroine's father leads a sally against the French beleaguering his fort, and hears in the mist his daughters trying to reach him—an episode hilariously criticized by Mark Twain. And of course, the acceptance of such conventions is not incompatible with realism. But in saying so, one is at once using that term in a special and limited sense.

If Pushkin is not realistic to the extent of observing a fidelity to appearance, still less is he concerned with probability. The intrigue depends upon a large initial coincidence, but probability is violated in other, more interesting, ways:

Suddenly the moon came out from behind the cloud and lighted a terrible sight. A gallows fixed to a raft was floating towards us. Three corpses were swinging on the cross-bar. A morbid curiosity possessed me. I wanted to look into the hanged men's faces. I told the oarsmen to hold the raft with a boat-hook, and my boat knocked against the floating gallows. I jumped out and found myself between the terrible posts. The full moon lighted the disfigured faces of the unfortunate creatures . . .

3

The episode is not included for its own sake. One of the hanged men is found by Grinyov, the narrator, to be one of his father's servants. And, as thus alarming Grinyov, the episode contributes smoothly enough to the main action. But the contribution is not a necessary contribution, and is in fact so slight that the passage, with its emphases—'morbid curiosity', 'the full moon', 'disfigured faces'—will at first be taken as simply a horrific set-piece. But it is not that either. 'Morbid curiosity', in Pushkin's prose, can be allowed to carry full weight, to refer at once to the jaded ennui of his so-called Byronic characters, of which Eugene Onegin is only the best known. Shvabrin, the only 'Byronic' character in *The Captain's Daughter*, is only sketched (though fairly condemned). But the history of Grinyov's relations with him before the fall of the fortress takes up such a reference as the 'morbid curiosity' here, to suggest a capacity for moral compromise in Grinyov. And such a suggestion is integral to the total organization of the tale.

For Pushkin's concern in *The Captain's Daughter* is a moral concern. And his realism must be construed to include an interest which is ideological, which can, with whatever looseness, be called 'philosophical'. Here the ideological theme is at its most insistent:

'Listen,' Pugatchov said, with a kind of wild inspiration, 'I will tell you a fairy-tale which in my childhood an old Calmuck woman told me. The eagle asked the raven one day: "Tell me, raven-bird, why do you live in the world for three hundred years and I only for thirty-three?"—"Because, father-eagle, you drink living blood," the raven said, "and I feed on things that are dead." The eagle thought "I will try and feed as he does." Very well. The eagle and the raven flew along. They saw the carcass of a horse, came down and perched on it. The raven plucked and praised the food. The eagle took a peck or two, then waved his wing and said: "No, brother raven, rather than feed on dead flesh for three hundred years, I would have one drink

4

of living blood—and leave the rest to God!" What do you think of the Calmuck tale?'

'It is clever,' I answered. 'But to live by murder and brigandage is, to my mind, just what plucking dead flesh means.'

The argument here is the argument of the whole tale. Pugatchov and his associates represent the impulsive appetite, an innate barbarian grandeur.[1] Grinyov is here made the spokesman of the opposing code, of order and tradition, a code represented more usually, however, by his father, by his general, and by Captain Mironov, his garrison-commander. The Russian military and patriotic tradition is here a moral symbol, precisely as the tradition of the British Merchant Service was a moral symbol for Conrad. Moreover the two codes, represented by Pugatchov on the one side and by Mironov on the other, could, it is plain, comprehensibly be described, in view of the period at which the tale was written, as 'Romantic' and 'Classical' respectively. In that light the passage is related to the general direction of all Pushkin's work, evident repeatedly at specific moments in his verse, where that takes up simultaneously the whole of two traditions, of Byron and Chenier on the one hand, of Parny and Voltaire on the other. And it is the consciousness in Pushkin of the two traditions, and of the necessity of judging between them, which invites the comparison with Goethe, and justifies the acknowledgement of Pushkin as a 'European artist'.

I do not mean to imply, however, that the passage about the Calmuck tale contains, in any usual sense, the 'moral' of *The Captain's Daughter*, a hard kernel of foreign matter at the centre. On the contrary, it represents only the most explicit phase of an argument which is the substance of the plot, and which is never, in fact, decided. For the sake of an early kind-

---

[1] 'I cannot describe how affected I was by this peasant song about the gallows, sung by men doomed to the gallows. Their menacing faces, their tuneful voices, the mournful expression they gave to the words expressive enough in themselves—it all thrilled me with a feeling akin to awe.'

ness, Pugatchov helps Grinyov to save the woman he loves, though both of them are connected with the loyalist forces opposing Pugatchov. Grinyov is forced, therefore, to feel, in some degree, a divided allegiance:

'And yet a strange feeling poisoned my joy: I could not help being troubled at the thought of the villain smeared with the blood of so many innocent victims and now awaiting his punishment. "Why didn't he fall on a bayonet: or get hit with a cannon-ball?" I thought with vexation. "He could not have done anything better." What will you have? I could not think of Pugatchov without remembering how he had spared me at one of the awful moments of my life and saved my betrothed from the vile Shvabrin's hands.'

But the explanation offered, in terms of the plot, does not exhaust Grinyov's feeling of guilt, of complicity, with regard to Pugatchov. This is certain. How otherwise explain Grinyov's foreshadowing dream, described while Pugatchov is still anonymous, and before Grinyov has contracted any obligations towards him?

'I was in that state of mind when reality gives way to dreams and merges into them in the shadowy visions of oncoming sleep. It seemed to me the storm was still raging and we were still wandering in the snowy desert. . . . Suddenly I saw a gateway and drove into the courtyard of our estate. My first thought was fear lest my father should be angry with me for my involuntary return and regard it as an intentional disobedience. Anxious, I jumped down from the chaise and saw my mother who came out to meet me on the steps, with an air of profound grief. "Don't make any noise," she said. "Your father is ill; he is dying and wants to say good-bye to you." Terror-stricken, I followed her to the bedroom. It was dimly lighted; people with sad-looking faces were standing by the bed. I approached the bed quietly; my mother lifted the bed-curtains and said: "Andrey Petrovitch! Petrusha has come; he returned when he heard of your illness; bless him." I knelt down and looked at the sick man. But what did I see? Instead of my father a black-bearded peasant lay on the bed looking at me merrily. I turned to my mother in perplexity and said to her: "What does it mean? This is not my father. And why should I ask this peasant's blessing?"... "Never mind, Petrusha," my mother answered, "he takes your father's place for the wedding; kiss his hand and he will bless you...." I would not do it. Then the peasant jumped off the bed, seized an axe from behind his back, and began waving it about. I wanted to run away and could not; the room was full of dead bodies; I stumbled against them and slipped in the pools of blood.... The terrible peasant called to me kindly, saying: "Don't be afraid, come and let me bless you." Terror and confusion possessed me ...'

Now this passage cannot be a concession to 'atmosphere', a horrific indulgence. For the effect is not appalling, but profoundly disturbing, in a way which was to be characteristic of Russian fiction, and which depends upon the simultaneous presence of discordant elements. Grinyov's mother has 'an air of profound grief'; Grinyov is 'terror-stricken'. But the peasant 'lay on the bed looking at me *merrily*'. Grinyov 'slipped in the pools of blood'. But 'the terrible peasant called to me *kindly*'. So 'terror and confusion possessed me'. The incident perplexes and confuses the reader, as well as Grinyov. And one must suppose that the nightmare is intended to carry full weight, to convey to the reader that, in some sense more radical than the coils of plot, the savage peasant is Grinyov's father, that Grinyov does require his blessing, and that when at the end Grinyov is brought to trial he is on trial almost like Kafka's 'K', ignorant of the cause he must plead, the offence with which he is charged. It does not much matter how the indebtedness is rationalized. Once can imagine the Marxist critic, who would make an obvious case on the grounds that Pugatchov is a peasant and/or the representative of a racial minority. The quite special status of the Cossack on both these counts would, as a fact of history, require some manipulation. More important, such a crucial passage as the address of Grinyov's father to his repentant serfs is far too much in character to be taken as evidence:

> 'My father went out on the steps to talk to them. When the peasants saw him they knelt down. "Well, you silly fools," he said to them, "whatever did you rebel for?".'

And the same is true of the only passage which could be supposed relevant to the problem of minorities, Grinyov's pious retrospective complacency over the mutilation of the captive Bashkir:

> 'When I recall that this happened in my lifetime and that now I have lived to see the gentle reign of the Emperor Alexander, I cannot but marvel at the rapid progress of enlightenment and the diffusion of humane principles. Young man! If my notes ever fall into your hands, remember that the best and most permanent changes are those due to the softening of manners and morals and not to any violent upheavals.'

On the whole I do not think one can or should rationalize Grinyov's indebtedness to Pugatchov and the Cossacks, except in so far as the latter, on the evidence of the Calmuck tale and the gallows-song, seem to 'stand for' the life of passionate impulse and barbarian grandeur. The plot seems to imply that the quite different tradition of civility arises out of barbarian values and is nourished by them.

It will certainly be argued that if Grinyov's trial is a real trial, valid outside the terms of the plot, then his release by the *dea ex machina*, the Empress, is a gross shelving of the issues raised. The fairy-tale convention, though, is consistent from first to last. The intrigue starts with a coincidence which has all the air of 'once upon a time . . .' and the denouement, the interview with the Empress, has the casual abruptness of the fairy godmother's waving of the wand. The whole tale, in short, is set firmly within a frame. It is highly conventional throughout. What remains within all the conventions, and in

8

conjunction with the moral argument, is Pushkin's realism. And the nature of that realism it is now not hard to see. Grinyov is realistically drawn, is no Faustian or Promethean prototype, serving to symbolize in his own conflicts the extreme conflicts of mankind. He is, on the contrary, a Russian country gentleman of the eighteenth century, conducting his internal argument at no more than normal intensity, with no more than normal honesty and courage. As such, he may be allowed to embody an ideological conflict, but not to resolve the conflict, nor to push it to the limit. He is no more, in many ways, than David Copperfield, but seen with much less indulgence, much more seriously. Characteristically, Pushkin's apparent *naïveté* masks, in the end, an effect of extreme sophistication:

'The memoirs of Pyotr Andreyitch Grinyov end at this point. It is known from the family tradition that he was released from confinement at the end of 1774, at the express order of the Empress; that he was present at the execution of Pugatchov, who recognized him in the crowd and nodded to him a minute before his lifeless, bleeding head was held up before the people.'

The Captain's Daughter is in no sense a difficult work. Except for the reader who has been invited to consider it as 'realistic', a description which is, in any other than a very special and limited sense, inappropriate, the tale insists upon being read with all the stresses and patterns which I have found it necessary here to draw out at some length. Once it is so read, even the minor episodes are seen to serve the purpose of an inclusive pattern. The allusion to *David Copperfield*, for example, recalls an episode which is superficially Dickensian. Yet a moment's thought suffices to emphasize that in Pushkin's scheme the episode serves a purpose which is far indeed from that of Dickens. I mean the description of Grinyov's first encounter with Zurin, the officer of Hussars, when Grinyov, the raw recruit travelling to his first garrison, is misled by Zurin into drinking too much and to losing money at billiards and at play. Where Dickens (at his usual level) would have used the episode to evoke a facile sympathy for the raw youth at large in the bewildering world, and probably would have 'played up' Zurin either into a melodramatic villain, or (more probably) into a 'fantastic', in Pushkin's hands the story advises the reader of the presence of a moral weakness in both characters. And as both characters represent that tradition which is offered by Pushkin as his 'moral positive', it further enlightens the reader that his author does not see the thing of which he approves through any rose tints, but critically, cautiously, and with reservations. Pugatchov, on the other hand, representing the other term in the moral problem, is seen with the same honesty. For he is almost at once presented in his worst light, at the bloody execution in the captured loyalist settlement. More complex than either is the delightful account of the council of war in Orenburg. Grinyov, as having personal experience of Pugatchov, is invited to attend the discussion held in Orenburg about the measures to be taken to meet the advancing rebels. He advises attack, an open engagement outside the walls. The cautious burghers prefer defence, caution and bribery. The general, being called upon to decide, admits his sympathy with the views of Grinyov, but submits to pressure and adopts the advice of the civilians. There is implicit criticism of the general, again the representative of what the reader is invited to approve. But more subtly (because Grinyov, the narrator, is obviously unaware of any moral compromise upon his part) there is criticism of Grinyov too. For the reader is not allowed to forget that it is in Grinyov's interest to advise the more dashing course of action, since the girl he loves is in the hands of his rival, behind the rebel lines.

The difficulties which face the English reader of Pushkin are very considerable. Pushkin was well-read in English literature, and the English reader continually comes across conventions from English writers, adopted by Pushkin, but modified by him, until they are almost (but not quite) unrecognizable.

Here, in *The Captain's Daughter*, the conventions are those of Walter Scott. But Pushkin, through his rigorous economy in style and composition, has so far changed the methods he took from Scott that to the English reader the conventions governing the story seem something wholly strange. So, in 'Eugene Onegin', the English reader will discern the influences of Byron and, perhaps, of Sterne. So, in other parts of Pushkin's prose-writing, the English reader comes across conventions adopted from the tale of terror. But this discernment in the reader may prove to be more of a hindrance than a help. For in nearly every case Pushkin improves upon his models, using conventions which were originally arbitrary and frivolous, for the discussion of a serious moral problem. Is there, for instance, any novel by Scott in which the moral issue is seen so clearly, the literary instrument used so honestly, as in Pushkin's self-effacing 'romance'?

II

THE HEART OF MIDLOTHIAN

꙰꙰꙰꙰꙰꙰꙰꙰꙰꙰꙰꙰꙰꙰꙰꙰꙰꙰꙰꙰꙰꙰꙰꙰꙰꙰꙰꙰꙰꙰

THERE is a patent connection between *The Captain's Daughter* and one of Scott's novels. When Pushkin's story was first translated into English,[1] George Saintsbury was quick to seize upon it, in order to damn with faint praise:

> These tales are really attractive enough, especially by reason of the odd simplicity which seems characteristic of Russian story. Except in manner, there is nothing very original about them; indeed, the last scene of the first and longest story, 'The Captain's Daughter', is, to use a very mild word, borrowed from Jeanie Deans' interview with Queen Caroline.[2]

Pushkin, writing for a Russian society which was avidly devouring the Waverley novels as they came out (and also the novels of Fenimore Cooper) was plainly and consciously challenging this comparison with *The Heart of Midlothian*.

The Heart of Midlothian is nowadays in better repute than any other of Scott's novels, and Robin Mayhead voices influential opinion when he is prepared to salvage this book alone from the body of Scott's *oeuvre*.[2] Even at that, he can

---

[1] *A Russian Romance*, translated by Mrs. J. Buchan Telfer (*née* Mouravieff), 1873.

[2] *The Academy*, May 29, 1875.

[3] Robin Mayhead, ' "The Heart of Midlothian": Scott as Artist', *Essays in Criticism*, Vol. VI, No. 3. July 1956.

really respect only the first half of the book, and in fact his case for a 'deeply pondered and carefully worked-out theme'—the nature of human justice—can't be endorsed even so. (The case could be better argued, surely, with *Redgauntlet*.) Joan Pittock, rejecting Mr. Mayhead's case,[1] reveals how low Scott's reputation has sunk when she decides that nevertheless '*The Heart of Midlothian* emerges as Scott's best novel', simply because 'Scott's own national antiquarian and legal interests were called more constantly, more powerfully (but not, on the whole, more coherently and significantly) into play than elsewhere.'

If this is the best that can be done for Scott, we might as well forget about him altogether. In fact, however, though there may be more of Scott in this novel than in any other, it is far from being his best.

In the first place the narration is insufferably orotund:

> The careful father was absent in his well-stocked byre, foddering those useful and patient animals on whose produce his living depended, and the summer evening was beginning to close in, when Jeanie Deans began to be very anxious for the appearance of her sister, and to fear that she would not reach home before her father returned from the labour of the evening . . .
>
> (Chapter X)

Or again:

> Some weeks intervened before Mr. Middleburgh, agreeably to his benevolent resolution, found an opportunity of taking a walk towards St. Leonard's, in order to discover whether it might be possible to obtain the evidence hinted at in the anonymous letter respecting Effie Deans.
>
> (Chapter XVIII)

Of course this sort of thing is always to be feared in Scott, but here it runs to an extreme. 'In order to discover whether it

[1] Joan H. Pittock, in 'The Critical Forum', *Essays in Criticism*, Vol. VII, No. 4. October 1957.

might be possible to obtain' (i.e. 'to see if he could get')—a little of this (and these are salient but fair examples of the narrative prose as a whole) does a lot of damage. One begins to suspect that Pushkin worked at *The Heart of Midlothian* in a spirit not far short of parody. For Pushkin, however imperfect his command of English, wasn't likely to respect an author who wrote 'those useful and patient animals on whose produce his living depended', when what he meant was 'his cows'. It is the less likely because what marks Pushkin's work as a whole, in verse and prose alike, is its extreme economy, the stripped severity of outline. There is a striking example of this in precisely the parallel which is too conspicuous to be missed, the similarity between Marya Ivanovna's interview with the Empress, and Jeanie Deans' interview with Queen Caroline. The two scenes have too much in common to leave it in doubt that the Scott episode was Pushkin's model in an unusually deliberate and immediate way. And this throws into relief the one large change that Pushkin introduces, the absence from his story of any intermediary such as John, Duke of Argyle in the novel by Scott. By thus removing the one element needed for plausibility and verisimilitude, Pushkin makes the whole matter of the royal interview like something in a fairy-story or a dream; and the Empress stands forth unashamedly as a *dea ex machina*. The ruthless elimination of superfluities is Pushkin's controlling principle alike in the framing of plot and in the framing of sentences—as can be detected even when we read translations.

To see how far Scott is from any such rigour in style, one need go no further than to a passage which Mr. Mayhead picks out for particular approval:

In former times, England had her Tyburn, to which the devoted victims of justice were conducted in solemn procession up what is now called Oxford Road. In Edinburgh, a large open street, or rather oblong square, surrounded by high houses, called the Grassmarket, was used for the same melancholy purpose. It was not ill-chosen for such a scene, being of consider-able extent, and therefore fit to accommodate a greater number of spectators, such as were usually assembled by this melancholy spectacle. On the other hand, few of the houses which surround it were, even in early times, inhabited by persons of fashion; so that those likely to be offended or over deeply affected by such unpleasant exhibitions were not in the way of having their quiet disturbed by them. The houses in the Grassmarket are, generally speaking, of a mean description; yet the place is not without some features of grandeur, being overhung by the southern side of the huge rock on which the castle stands, and by the moss-grown battlements and turreted walls of that ancient fortress.

Mr. Mayhead observes, 'One cannot miss the irony of that phrase, "the devoted victims of justice".' But there can be little doubt that Scott missed it, since 'devoted' means what it meant for Milton, not what it means today, and it is regularly used by Scott (and by Fenimore Cooper) as an inert makeweight, one of the heedless Latinisms which pepper their staple styles, and have no more function there than just to impart a hollow dignity. In this passage 'melancholy purpose', slackly echoed by 'melancholy spectacle' at the end of the next sentence, is proof of how far Scott was from inviting the sort of attention which Mr. Mayhead exhorts us to give. 'Melancholy' is used twice, and yet in neither case is it doing enough work to be used once. To anyone who still believes that 'the essential technique in an art that works by using words is the way in which words are used'[1] it may as well be said at once that Scott in his prose never uses words so as to invite attention of Mr. Mayhead's sort. Still, Scott's style in *The Heart of Midlothian* is exceptionally slack. And so it is likely that such of Scott as contributed substantially to *The Captain's Daughter* came from other novels where the style is incomparably cleaner and firmer.

And not just the style, but the narrative structure also. For the plot of *The Heart of Midlothian* is a tissue of improbabil-

[1] Q. D. Leavis, *Fiction and the Reading Public*, p. 233.

ities and coincidences. So is the plot of Pushkin. But Pushkin makes no bones about it; rather, he deliberately heightens the unreality so as to establish firmly a frame of convention for us to enter into, the convention of the fairy-story or folk-tale. This, as we have seen, is the effect of not providing any figure to correspond to Scott's Duke of Argyle. Scott on the other hand tries to paper over the implausibilities, and conceal them. It is Scott, not Pushkin, who is the 'realist'. And so the implausibilities infect what is or should have been the central action. As in better novels by Scott, the central action in *The Heart of Midlothian* is tied to a turning-point in history, the revolutionary change from Scotland before the Union to Scotland after it. But whereas in *The Captain's Daughter* one person, the central character (made susceptible and wavering for the purpose) is torn between this past and this future, in *The Heart of Midlothian* it is a family that is thus torn apart, not a person but a group of persons. And since one of these persons, Jeanie Deans, has to be 'strong', her sister Effie has to be not just 'weak' but, to counterbalance her sister, so extremely weak that her weakness cannot be motivated nor accounted for by any features of temperament or environment. And in fact Scott never even attempts to justify or explain this weakness, not by analysis nor (and this is more damaging) by any direct presentation. Effie's susceptibility, on which the whole action turns, is not even defined, not even described, let alone analysed or accounted for.

And yet of course there are distinguished things in Scott's novel, and things which have a direct bearing on Pushkin. A recent critic has remarked:

It is one of the ironies of literature that Scott should have been taken for a pioneer of romanticism—indeed, should have actually been one, on the Continent especially. For touch his mind at any point and set it against any of the basic trends of true romanticism, and the two will at once appear to be in flat opposition. The cult of wild Nature?—he said himself that he had no eye for the picturesque in scenery. Human beings came first for him; rocks, mountains, trees and waterfalls were very bad seconds. The cult of the ego?—he despised the autobiographical, what he called the age's 'desire, or rather rage, for literary anecdote and private history'; and although he liked Byron and admired his verse, he deplored and hated the Byronic exhibitionism. The cult of the unconscious?—he was a man of common sense, of the conscious and controlling will. The cult of sentiment, of the Man of Feeling?—'of all sorts of parade', he wrote to Maria Edgeworth, 'I think the parade of feeling and sentiment the most disgusting'. The cult of the individualist genius, the law unto himself?—again and again he asserts that the writer should be and live like other men, accept their responsibilities and live by their standards. He was no romantic; he was an Augustan, who brought to bear on romantic materials a mind humorous and worldly-wise, extrovert and sane.[1]

It will suffice for the moment to choose just one tendency of Romanticism which seems to me more 'basic' than any of those here listed, and to set Scott against it. This is the Romanticism of Wordsworth's tract on the Convention of Cintra:

The instincts of natural and social man; the deeper emotions; the simpler feelings; the spacious range of the disinterested imagination; the pride in country for country's sake, when to serve has not been a formal profession—and the mind is therefore left in a state of dignity only to be surpassed by having served nobly and generously; the instantaneous accomplishment in which they start up who, upon a searching call, stir for the land which they love—not from personal motives, but for a reward which is undefined and cannot be missed; the solemn fraternity which a great Nation composes—gathered together, in a stormy season, under the shade of ancestral feeling; the delicacy of moral honour which pervades the minds of a people, when despair has been suddenly thrown off and expectations are

[1] Patrick Cruttwell, 'Walter Scott', in *From Blake to Byron* (Pelican Guide to English Literature, Vol. 5), pp. 110–111.

lofty; the apprehensiveness to a touch unkindly or irreverent, where sympathy is at once exacted as a tribute and welcomed as a gift; the power of injustice and inordinate calamity to transmute, to invigorate, and to govern—to sweep away the barriers of opinion—to reduce under submission passions purely evil— to exalt the nature of indifferent qualities, and to render them fit companions for the absolute virtues with which they are summoned to associate—to consecrate passions which, if not bad in themselves, are of such temper that, in the calm of ordinary life, they are rightly deemed so—to correct and embody these passions—and, without weakening them (nay, with tenfold addition to their strength), to make them worthy of taking their place as the advanced guard of hope, when a sublime movement of deliverance is to be originated;—these arrangements and resources of nature, these ways and means of society, have so little connection with those others upon which a ruling minister of a long-established government is accustomed to depend; these—elements as it were of a universe, functions of a living body—are so opposite, in their mode of action, to the formal machine which it has been his pride to manage;—that he has but a faint perception of their immediate efficacy; knows not the facility with which they assimilate with other powers; nor the property by which such of them—as, from necessity of nature, must change or pass away—will, under wise and fearless management, surely generate lawful successors to fill their place when their appropriate work is performed.

It is a far call from this oratorical splendour to Scott in Chapter XXVIII of his novel, defending his countrymen against the imputation of clannishness. And yet Scott is surely appealing to and defining the same values:

The eagerness with which Scottish people meet, communicate, and, to the extent of their power, assist each other, although it is often objected to us as a prejudice and narrowness of sentiment, seems, on the contrary, to arise from a most justifiable and honourable feeling of patriotism, combined with a conviction which, if undeserved, would long since have been con-

futed by experience, that the habits and principles of the nation
are a sort of guarantee for the character of the individual. At any
rate, if the extensive influence of this national partiality be
considered as an additional tie, binding man to man, and calling
forth the good offices of such as can render them to the countryman who happens to need them, we think it must be found to
exceed, as an active and efficient motive to generosity, that more
impartial and wider principle of general benevolence, which we
have sometimes seen pleaded as an excuse for assisting no individual whatever.

This shows Scott explicitly preferring to the 'Augustan' tenet
of rational benevolence the unwritten and irrational laws of
usage, custom and habit. And it shows him thoroughly in tune
with at least one of 'the basic trends of true romanticism', a
trend which is as apparent in Wordsworth's 'Old Cumberland
Beggar' as in the Miltonic eloquence of his tract on the Convention of Cintra—'the solemn fraternity which a great Nation
composes—gathered together, in a stormy season, under the
shade of ancestral feeling; . . .' (The nation that Wordsworth
has particularly in view is not of course the English but the
Spanish nation.) This is not a 'cult' of this nor a 'cult' of that,
but a perception that the central fact of politics, and the guiding principle of all public and much private morality, is the
fact of community considered as a state of being or a state of
feeling. The name of Burke and the title of a work so strictly
and deliberately parochial as 'The Old Cumberland Beggar'—
these may suffice to distinguish this wisdom from the national-
istic chauvinism which is its perversion. And this is a wisdom
rediscovered by the Romantic movement, which both Pushkin
and Mickiewicz appreciated in Scott, which made him—thanks
to them and to others, and through no 'irony of literature'—
'a pioneer of romanticism . . . on the Continent especially'.

This is indeed implied in everything Scott writes, an assumption so basic that it is seldom explicit; and it gives value and
energy to *The Heart of Midlothian* as to much that is inferior

to that. For the sake of it, even his poorest novels repay the reading. Those who talk of Scott's 'humanity' say too little by asserting too much; but this sense of what the community is, a feeling of and for community, is a major constituent if it is not indeed the definitive distinction of what we apprehend too loosely as his 'humanity'. For Pushkin and Mickiewicz, because of the chronically bad relations between Poland and Russia, it was far more difficult, and at times it proved impossible, to prevent this feeling from being debased into chauvinism, its parody. Yet certainly this conviction that all are brothers, that the national community and even larger communities are at least potentially fraternities, is part of what lies behind Grinyov's dream about his peasant-father, as behind the elder Grinyov's address to his penitent serfs. It is part of the effect of the passage about the dream, however little we may be aware of it. And so one knows from *The Captain's Daughter* alone, and from that even in translation, that it is a travesty of Pushkin to say 'The brotherhood of man would have appealed to Pushkin, if he had thought about it at all, as an excellent subject for a satiric poem'.[1] This is a far worse perversion than that of those Stalinist critics who would make Pushkin seem to be saying this at times when he isn't. Pushkin shared with Scott the sense for what community is, and the conviction of its value; and this is enough to prove that *The Captain's Daughter* isn't after all a parody of Scott, however conscious Pushkin may have been, and doubtless was, of mak-

---

[1] E. J. Simmons. *Pushkin* (Oxford University Press, 1937), p. 5: 'one must not search for a moral in his works; his muse is truly on the side of both good and evil. There is no tendentiousness, no social teaching, no moral pathos. Although a sincere patriot, he was never a Slavophile, for intellectually he felt as much at home in the culture of Europe as in that of his own country. He opposed evil, but he never preached a crusade against it. . . . The brotherhood of man would have appealed to Pushkin, if he had thought about it at all, as an excellent subject for a satiric poem. As for purpose in art—he summed it all up in one phrase: the purpose of poetry is poetry.'

ing a terse elegance out of what in Scott was turgid, muffled and untidy.

Yet there is more to *The Captain's Daughter* than this, and in particular there is more to Grinyov's dream than this. To find it we shall need to look further into Scott than *The Heart of Midlothian*.

III

WAVERLEY

❦❦❦

IT is a long time now since anyone coupled the name of Scott, as Hazlitt and Ruskin did, with the name of Shakespeare. Yet to Pushkin and Mickiewicz this coupling would have been natural, and Pushkin in fact explicitly made the comparison. Writing in 1830, he declared:

> The principal charm of Walter Scott's novels lies in the fact that we are introduced to the past not through the *enflure* of French tragedies, not through the primness of sentimental novels, not through the *dignité* of history, but in a contemporary, domestic manner . . . *ce qui nous charme dans le roman historique —c'est ce qui est historique est absolument ce que nous voyons—* Shakespeare, Goethe, Walter Scott have no servile predilection for kings and heroes. . . .

And as for the name of Goethe in this connection, it is interesting that within a couple of years of Pushkin's making this connection, Mickiewicz, his one-time friend, was in his *Pan Tadeusz* combining the procedures of Goethe in *Hermann und Dorothea* with the procedures of Scott's *Waverley*. All this of course, and Pushkin's tribute to Scott, are couched in very general terms. I hope I may in a short while make the point with more particularity. And at least I venture to hope that, if we no longer listen to Hazlitt and Ruskin on Scott, we may listen to Mickiewicz and Pushkin.

22

Now, to be sure, reading what critics have to say of these Slavic writers, one would not readily imagine that either author held a high opinion of Scott, or drew on him to much purpose in their own writing. Prince Mirsky, for instance, writing of Pushkin's first attempt at the novel, *The Negro of Peter the Great*, which he left unfinished in 1828, applauds the first chapter as 'reminiscent of the French novelists of the eighteenth century rather than of Scott'. 'But', he goes on, 'the following chapters are over-encumbered with historical colour and all the antiquarianism dear to the heart of Sir Walter.' And he decides there is good reason to suppose that Pushkin abandoned the story precisely because he admired Scott as little as apparently Prince Mirsky does. Similarly, when he treats of Pushkin's completed novel *The Captain's Daughter*, having to note the very close affinity between the heroine's interview with the Empress and Jeanie Deans' interview with Queen Caroline at the end of *The Heart of Midlothian*, he hastens to remove the implied slur by declaring of Pushkin's story that nevertheless 'It is quite free from all antiquarianism, description, and bric-à-brac'. Prince Mirsky's attitude to Scott is clear, and it is one that is shared in the English-speaking countries: Scott clutters up his stories with antiquarian information and stagey properties which have no relation to his themes, those themes in fact being quite perfunctory, no more than convenient clothes-rails on which to hang the author's idiosyncratic hobbies. Rather similarly, Mr. Czeslaw Milosz, writing in the magazine *Encounter* about G. R. Noyes's version of *Pan Tadeusz*, decides '. . . all that remains of that extraordinary "novel in verse", whose characters move like the figures in a ballet, is the sort of plot one might find in Sir Walter Scott . . .' And here too we gather quite clearly that this is very little to be left with. The critic of Mickiewicz is at one with the critic of Pushkin in thinking they know better than either poet about the author the poets had chosen in some degree (and on this showing, how unfortunately) to imitate.

Scott, in the General Preface to the edition of 1829, tells how 'about the year 1805, I threw together about one third of the first volume of *Waverley*'. The MS. was shown to a friend who reported adversely upon it, and it was then abandoned for, it seems, about seven years. Scott was induced to take it up again partly by accident (he recalls finding the forgotten MS. when searching for fishing-tackle in an attic), but partly by design, in an attempt to emulate Maria Edgeworth:

> I felt that something might be attempted for my own country, of the same kind with that which Miss Edgeworth so fortunately achieved for Ireland—something which might introduce her natives to those of the sister kingdom, in a more favourable light than they had been placed in hitherto, and tend to procure sympathy for their virtues and indulgence for their foibles.

So far as Scott could remember, the portion completed in 1805 comprised only the first seven chapters. And if we re-read these with this in mind, the difference between these and those that follow is very obvious. It is a difference of kind, not of degree. The writing of these chapters is as accomplished as in the rest, but in a different convention. It is stiff and weighty, and Augustan; it is within measurable distance of, for instance, Jane Austen's *Mansfield Park*:

> His resolution of marriage had been adopted in a fit of indignation; the labour of courtship did not quite suit the dignified indolence of his habits; he had but just escaped the risk of marrying a woman who could never love him, and his pride could not be greatly flattered by the termination of his amour, even if his heart had not suffered.

At other times we are reminded not so much of *Mansfield Park* as of Fielding's *Amelia*; but at all events the writer of these earlier chapters is what the late eighteenth century called 'a moral writer'. His intention is not 'to procure sympathy' (that came later, as we have seen, from Miss Edgeworth) but to judge and discriminate. This is especially apparent in the treatment of the hero; the first seven chapters (especially Chapter III, 'Education', where, Scott tells us, he is describing his own boyhood through Waverley's) seem prepared to judge Waverley quite harshly, whereas in the novel as a whole he seems a person we are meant, on the whole, to respect. And yet perhaps it would be truer to say that in the story as a whole the question of how far we respect the hero just does not arise. In fact, it is precisely in thus inducing the reader to suspend judgement that Scott's momentous innovation consists; the value of this effect, and the means of achieving it, were I believe precisely what Pushkin and Mickiewicz seized upon. This is something different from for instance Fielding's treatment of *Tom Jones*. We are invited to be indulgent to Fielding's hero. But we are asked to feel that this indulgence is right and natural; and Tom is finally held up for admiration, judged and gloriously acquitted. Pushkin's Grinyov and Mickiewicz's Tadeusz are, like Edward Waverley, obscurely likeable young men of no particular distinction, whom we neither judge nor wish to judge. And if Scott had in fact any predecessors in this, I don't think we need look further than where he points us, to the Irish novelist Maria Edgeworth, who made the discovery in *Castle Rackrent* but chose never to develop it. And this is one reason for dwelling on the gap in the writing of *Waverley*, because between the writing before the intermission and after it we can see the discovery being made.

Again, Chapter I is a humorous disquisition, rather ponderous but effective enough, on the implications of Scott's subtitle, *'Tis Sixty Years Since*, and on the sort of novel *Waverley* might have been, had it been subtitled differently. It might have been *Waverley, a Tale of other Days* (that is, a Gothic novel like Mrs. Radcliffe's *Udolpho*, the favourite reading of Pushkin's heroine in *Dubrovsky*); or it might have been *Waverley, a Romance from the German* (that is, a tale of terror, like that fictitious one in which one of Mickiewicz's characters is proud to have figured, *The Count, or the Mysteries of the Castle of*

Birbante-Rocca); or it might have been, Scott says, a 'Sentimental Tale'; or, finally, 'A Tale of the Times'. Scott maintains that, by casting his story sixty years earlier, he forfeits on the one hand the appeal of the topical, on the other hand the appeal of the antique and the remote. And he claims to make the best of this by writing a novel not of manners but of men:

> Considering the disadvantages inseparable from this part of my subject, I must be understood to have resolved to avoid them as far as possible, by throwing the force of my narrative upon the characters and passions of the actors;—those passions common to men in all stages of society, and which have alike agitated the human heart, whether it throbbed under the steel corselet of the fifteenth century, the brocaded coat of the eighteenth, or the blue frock and white dimity waistcoat of the present day. Upon these passions it is no doubt true that the state of manners and laws casts a necessary colouring; but the bearings, to use the language of heraldry, remain the same, though the tincture may be not only different, but opposed in strong contradistinction.

This constitutes a plea for the thoroughly neo-classical principle that the business of the artist is with 'nature', meaning by that the constant elements in human nature to be detected beneath the adventitious distinctions of period, race and trade. And certainly this profession fits well enough the first seven chapters; if it fits the rest, it does so much less plainly. At any rate one must say, using Scott's metaphor, that in the rest of the book far more attention is given to the 'tincture' than is apparent at the start. And it is, I suppose, one of the most serious questions that can be asked of the whole *Waverley* series, whether in these novels Scott believes in a constant 'nature' in this sense, or not. Mr. Duncan Forbes believes he does; Professor Trevelyan declared he does not.

At any rate, the clearest indication that Scott resumed his novel with a different intention is the fact that some of the features derided in Chapter I, as stock properties of the kind of novel he did not intend to write, in fact appear in the novel he *did* write. Thus 'the jocularity of a clownish but faithful valet' is adduced as one of the few features of light relief permissible to the Gothic novel; yet the later chapters of *Waverley* present more than one such figure. And similarly the 'Sentimental Tale', according to Scott, requires 'a heroine with a profusion of auburn hair, and a harp, the soft solace of her solitary hours, which she fortunately finds always the means of transporting from castle to cottage'; in *Waverley* Flora MacIvor has dark hair, but apart from that this business with the harp appears with all solemnity in the sentimental tableau of Chapter XXII, 'Highland Minstrelsy'. This chapter is an Ossianic indulgence on Scott's part, and a weakness in the book though not an important one. Neither Mickiewicz's Telimena nor the heroine of Pushkin's *Dubrovsky* are harpists, but they are permitted to take up romantically interesting postures in the open air, and it is notable that both authors make them far more aware of what they are doing than Scott does with his Flora, and both Pushkin and Mickiewicz are ironically detached and wary about this decorative femininity as Scott is not. As for the 'clownish but faithful valet', this tradition dies hard. Pushkin's version of this figure is Savelyich in *The Captain's Daughter*, a character who habitually gets from the critics far more attention than he deserves from his relatively marginal function in the economy of the story as a whole. But the worst case of the clownish valet is Andrew Fairservice in *Rob Roy*.

As for *Waverley*, one important and unexpected feature of this novel is the way it profits from the seven years' gap in Scott's writing of it. For although the difference between the writing of 1805 and the rest stands out very plainly when we know to look for it, it does not jar on the reader who knows nothing about it. On the contrary it has a powerful effect on him without his noticing it. For as it happens Scott broke off the first writing at just the point where Waverley moves out of English into Scottish society; and the change in attitude and style thus corresponds with the change of social milieu, contributing at once something to the different atmosphere that Scott at this point needs to create. The formality and sedateness of the style of the first chapters reflects just those qualities in English society; something fantastic and craggy in the writing when Scott resumes it (one thinks of Sterne now rather than Fielding) corresponds no less aptly to a quality he wants to bring out in the society of the Scots. One example of this will be enough.

Maria Edgeworth, responding to Scott's tribute in the Epilogue to *Waverley*, found only one criticism to make in the course of a full and elaborate examination:

> 'We were so possessed with the belief that the whole story and every character in it was real, that we could not endure the occasional addresses from the author to the reader. They are like Fielding: but for that reason we cannot bear them, we cannot bear that an author of such high powers, of such original genius, should for a moment stoop to imitation . . .'[1]

This objection is such as will appeal in quarters where it is still fashionable to dislike Thackeray for 'breathing down our necks'; and of course, coming from Miss Edgeworth, it carries weight. But I am not sure that it is fair:

> 'The ingenious licentiate, Francisco de Ubeda, when he commenced his history of La Picara Justina Diez,—which, by the way, is one of the most rare books of Spanish literature,— complained of his pen having caught up a hair, and forthwith begins, with more eloquence than common sense, an affectionate expostulation with that useful implement, upbraiding it with being the quill of a goose,—a bird inconstant by nature, as frequenting the three elements of water, earth, and air, indifferently, and being, of course, "to one thing constant never". Now I protest to thee, gentle reader, that I entirely dissent from Francisco de Ubeda in this matter, and hold it the most useful

[1] *Life and Letters of Maria Edgeworth*, ed. A. J. C. Hare, Vol. I, pp. 226–231.

quality of my pen, that it can speedily change from grave to gay, and from description and dialogue to narrative and character. So that if my quill display no other properties of its mother-goose than her mutability, truly I shall be well pleased; and I conceive that you, my worthy friend, will have no occasion for discontent. From the jargon, therefore, of the Highland gillies, I pass to the character of their Chief. It is an important examination, and therefore, like Dogberry, we must spare no wisdom.'

This, in its sprightliness, is more like Sterne than Fielding. It is surprising when it comes in the book, and as we read it we take it to be only an embarrassed apology that we could do without. Yet in fact, as we read on, we see that it sets the tone admirably for what follows, our first introduction to the personality and situation of the Highland chieftain, Fergus Mac-Ivor. Everything that is volatile, arbitrary, quaint, even exotic (the Spanish reference) is thoroughly in keeping with the situation and the personality of MacIvor and of others like him. Chapter XXIV begins in a similar way, and can also be justified, I think, though on different grounds.

It is plain, as I have said, that in 1814 Scott was prepared to regard such a character as Edward Waverley's far more leniently than when he first envisaged him in 1805. On the other hand, he is still recognizably the same person at the end of the book as at the beginning. And if Scott's attitude towards him has changed, he does not make the reader's attitude change at the turn of a page. The change of attitude to the hero is gradual and insidious; it is a drift through the whole book, not an abrupt change of front. In Chapter XXV, for instance, the flaws in Waverley's character are still insisted upon, as here, where he is contrasted with the Highland chieftain Fergus MacIvor:

... the bold and prompt habits of thinking, acting, and speaking, which distinguished this young Chieftain, had given him a considerable ascendancy over the mind of Waverley. Endowed with at least equal powers of understanding, and with much finer genius, Edward yet stooped to the bold and decisive activity of an intellect which was sharpened by the habit of acting on a preconceived and regular system, as well as by extensive knowledge of the world.

After this, Waverley's character is seen by the reader exclusively as it strikes off from, and appears in contrast to, Fergus MacIvor's. Each is the foil to the other. And by a management of great art, our attitude to Waverley changes as his attitude changes towards Fergus. As Waverley is gradually disillusioned with MacIvor, so we find more to esteem in Waverley. And, even more effectively, the development of our attitude towards him reflects the course of the whole rebellion which is fomented, breaks out and is quelled as the book draws on. In the first weeks of the insurrection, all our sympathies are with the intrepid Fergus, and Waverley seems only his inconstant shadow; on the march to Derby, as the Jacobite impetus gradually falls away, we esteem Waverley more and Fergus less. For, from the standpoint of 1745, Waverley represents the future and Fergus the past.

This is the meaning of the book, at its deepest and most affecting level. It shows the victory of the un-heroic (the English Waverley) over the heroic (the Scottish MacIvor); it shows that this was inevitable and on the whole welcome, yet also sad. This complex balanced attitude towards the historical turning-point is maintained, above all, by the fine stroke (in a sense the clue to the whole book) of making both the representative of the heroic attitude, and his counterpart, the representative of the un-heroic, flawed characters. The Baron Bradwardine is a more estimable representative of Scottish heroism than MacIvor is; Colonel Talbot is a more admirable representative of the unheroic English than Waverley is. Yet MacIvor and Waverley are in the centre of the picture; Talbot and the Baron support only the two main figures.

'Heroic' and 'un-heroic' may both be misunderstood, unless we admit that for 'heroic' we may substitute 'barbarian', for 'un-heroic', 'civilized'. The second pair of terms tilts the scales of approval towards the English, as the first pair towards the Scots; the novelist's achievement is in tilting neither way, but holding the balance scrupulously steady. Certainly by calling Waverley and Talbot 'un-heroic' we do not mean that they are anything but brave; both *are* brave, as Scott is at some pains to insist. The real distinction perhaps is that for MacIvor and Bradwardine the principle governing all conduct is the barbarian heroic principle of 'honour'; for Waverley and Talbot it is something else, reasonableness, public spirit, justice, or 'the greatest happiness of the greatest number'. Of all the characters Colonel Philip Talbot is presented as the most nearly perfect; yet he is made to justify the punitive measures after Culloden, and on grounds only speciously 'moral', really utilitarian, to excuse the quite random justice that pardoned Bradwardine and beheaded poor Evan Dhu. The question at issue is brought to a head very well when Talbot reports on his intercession on behalf of the Baron:

'Thus you see *my* prince can be as generous as *yours*. I do not pretend, indeed, that he conveys a favour with all the foreign graces and compliments of your Chevalier errant; but he has a plain English manner, and the evident reluctance with which he grants your request, indicates the sacrifice which he makes of his own inclination to your wishes.'

(Is it going beyond our brief to point out that in thus acceding the Elector abandoned his own honour, no less than both Talbot's and Waverley's? No principle governs his actions, which are entirely arbitrary, like the acts of a despot. He does what he believes to be unjust, and makes the intercessors share the guilt and the responsibility.)

Inevitably Scott feels nostalgia for the heroism that the passing of time has destroyed. And this nostalgia, when it comes to overt expression, is all the more just and affecting because the author has shown himself, in treating of MacIvor, well aware of the dangerous and discreditable aspects of the heroic attitude. Here is the Baron Bradwardine after the rebellion is over and he has been pardoned, but is still homeless:

A natural sigh closed the sentence; but the quiet equanimity with which the Baron endured his misfortunes, had something in it venerable, and even sublime. There was no fruitless repining, no turbid melancholy; he bore his lot, and the hardships which it involved, with a good-humoured, though serious composure, and used no violent language against the prevailing party.

'I did what I thought my duty', said the good old man, 'and questionless they are doing what they think theirs. It grieves me sometimes to look upon these blackened walls of the house of my ancestors; but doubtless officers cannot always keep the soldier's hand from depredation and spuilzie; and Gustavus Adolphus himself as ye may read in Colonel Munro his Expedition with the worthy Scotch regiment called Mackay's regiment, did often permit it.—Indeed I have myself seen as sad sights as Tully-Veolan now is, when I served with the Marechal Duke of Berwick. To be sure we may say with Virgilius Maro, *Fuimus Troes*—and there's the end of an auld sang. But houses and families and men have a' stood lang eneuch when they have stood till they fall with honour; and now I hae gotten a house that is not unlike a *domus ultima*'—they were now standing below a steep rock. 'We poor Jacobites', continued the Baron, looking up, 'are now like the conies in Holy Scripture (which the great traveller Pococke called Jerboa), a feeble people, that make our abode in the rocks. So, fare you well, my good lad, till we meet at Janet's in the even; for I must get into my Patmos, which is no easy matter for my auld stiff limbs.'

The noble poignancy here ('houses and families and men have a' stood lang eneuch when they have stood till they fall with honour') depends upon the pedantry that stands around it. This pedantry is in character; but its purpose is at this point no longer just to make the figure of the Baron picturesque and individual. It is what makes this passage elegiac, rather than nostalgic. The references, Scriptural, military, classical, build up a picture not just of one man's spiritual world, but of a whole society. The same ranges of reference come together in a Presbyterian poet like Alexander Hume in the sixteenth century; they belong to a Scottish cultural tradition, transcending distinctions of political or religious allegiance, which was destroyed in 1745. The reference to Virgil is particularly pregnant. The Baron is always translating Latin tags, as here with 'there's the end of an auld sang', into the racy and colloquial Scots language of his time; and in consequence the society he laments is seen to be Augustan in the strict sense, that is to say, appealing to the Rome of Augustus as a model of civilization, every bit as earnestly as the more notoriously Augustan society of London under Queen Anne. 'There's the end of an auld sang' is a translation of 'Fuimus Troes' only in the specially free sense in which Pope's *Imitations of Horace* are translations of Horace. All this, by giving the nostalgic feeling something precise and articulated on which to work, takes the passage out of the realm of the nostalgic as commonly understood, and makes it elegiac, something of a stately ritual, clear-sighted, composed, and sad rather than melancholy— like the state of mind of the Baron himself.

Nothing less and nothing different, I think, should be said of some passages from Mickiewicz's *Pan Tadeusz*, such as this:

> The Lithuanian judge
> Offers by way of reproof
> To the young Pan Tadeusz
> Decorum, the difficult science,
> No matter of graceful posture
> Or ease at the affable counter,
> But bearing of old Poland;
> Courtesy, being extended
> To all, not without distinction
> But in the mode most proper,
> As to master with man, or to children
> With parents, or each to each

In public husband and wife.
'Discourse in noble mansions
Was then a persistent history,
And talk among the gentry
The annals of their provinces;
Gentlemen watched their step,
Knowing such pains were taken
To judge of their deserving;
But neither name nor stock
Associates nor achievements
Are now enquired after,
And each goes where he pleases
Short of the known informer
And the scrounger by profession.
Vespasian never questioned
Out of what hands his riches
Came to him, having decided
Money was "not to be sniffed at".
So men approve a title
And value their connections
By current estimates,
As if to strike up a friendship
Were also a transaction.
But a sense of personal worth
Is arrived at only by weighing;
The beam is only plumb
With a counterpoise in the pan,
A worthiness in another.'

If we recall the accent of living speech and dialectal modifica-
tion in the passage from Scott, we doubtless get some idea of
what we have lost in translation. But the Judge's allusion to
Vespasian seems to function in just the same way as Bradwardine's reference to Virgil—except that, as always, there is
an added edge to the Polish specimen, that comes of Poland's
being, and feeling herself to be down the centuries, on the
embattled frontier of Christendom and the Latin world. This

affinity once recognized, the points of comparison multiply. Scott's Scotland, like Mickiewicz's Lithuania, is the seat of a provincial culture which has, so each writer persuades us, all the virtues of the provincial—a slow and steady tempo as against the whirl of fad and fashion in the metropolis, St. Petersburg or London; social communities bound together organically by usage and unwritten law as against blue-print regimentation from above; personal idiosyncrasies allowed to flower into eccentricities or harmless obsessions instead of being ironed out or else aggravated into perversions. These provinces escape, on the other hand, the vices of the provincial, being 'out of touch', parochial or complacent, only in indifferent matters, having in essential things a direct channel clear and running, back to the well springs of European culture. Mickiewicz's judge is a lawyer of sorts, but his pedantry has not a specifically legal flavour, any more than Bradwardine's. However Scott, himself a lawyer, is fond of introducing characters like Bartoline Saddletree in *The Heart of Midlothian* or Peter Peebles in *Redgauntlet*, who are pedants of the law; and in *Pan Tadeusz* Mickiewicz, the son of a lawyer, has at least one such character, the Apparitor. What is more, at his best (which is to say, in *Redgauntlet* rather than *The Heart of Midlothian*), this pedantry in Scott throws an oblique light on the central theme, which is precisely the question of the rule of law in a society where loyalties are legitimately divided. And this is a main concern of *Pan Tadeusz*, too, in all that is related to its subtitle, the *Last Foray in Lithuania*. Mickiewicz's treatment is comic, where Scott's at least in *Redgauntlet*, which is one of his most sombre books, is tragic in feeling. Indeed, when one comes to think of it, everything in Mickiewicz's poem which concern the Foray and the vengeful intrigues of the old squire Gerwazy is an exact parallel to the Jacobitism of *Waverley*, in that it represents the barbaric principle of honour surviving from feudal society into an era which demands rather the rule of law; and between the two bodies of sentiment Mickiewicz's feelings appear to be divided as equally as Scott's. The balance is held just as steadily, though perhaps the use of the comic mode makes this impartiality rather easier for Mickiewicz than for Scott.

There are many other elements which *Pan Tadeusz* and *Waverley* have in common, and of course we mustn't lose sight of the possibility that some of these derive from a common source in what one can only call 'the spirit of the age'. But there is one other common element which cannot be allowed to pass unremarked. This is 'the man of feeling'. In *Waverley*, one is made to realize how irretrievably the old Scotland has disappeared, by the master-stroke of giving the dedication of the work at the end—'To our Scottish Addison, Henry Mackenzie'. Mackenzie, author of the novel called *The Man of Feeling*, was or seemed to be the author of much more, of a new type of individual and a new moral paragon, the man who prided himself most on his susceptibility, more on his tender heart than his level head. And Scott is quite sincere of course—he really esteems the new Scottish culture (though it is Anglo-Scottish by this time), which has come to replace the old and is represented by 'the man of feeling' in Boswell's *Hypochondriack* and Burns's letters no less than in Mackenzie himself. In this new Scotland of Henry Mackenzie the criterion of behaviour is no longer objective at all, neither barbaric honour nor the greatest happiness of the greatest number, but subjective, the intensity of one's own emotional reactions.

If anyone thinks that this is to read too much into Scott's story, they would do well to read Chapter LII, and Flora Mac-Ivor's prophecy of what Waverley will become in later life:

> I will tell you where he will be at home, my dear, and in his place,—in the quiet circle of domestic happiness, lettered indolence, and elegant enjoyments, of Waverley-Honour. And he will refit the old library in the most exquisite Gothic taste, and garnish its shelves with the rarest and most valuable volumes; and he will draw plans and landscapes, and write verses, and rear

temples, and dig grottoes;—and he will stand in a clear summer night in the colonnade before the hall, and gaze on the deer as they stray in the moonlight, or lie shadowed by the boughs of the huge old fantastic oaks;—and he will repeat verses to his beautiful wife, who will hang upon his arm;—and he will be a happy man.

Here is the man of feeling already—in 1745! Scott takes pains to show that Miss MacIvor is an exceptionally intelligent woman, but she must needs be extraordinary indeed to divine that the taste of the next half-century was to be 'exquisite Gothic'. For Waverley in 1745 is the man of the future. The 'man of feeling' was just emerging on to the stage of history (Shenstone perhaps was the prototype) but it was a full generation later, in the time of Uvedale Price, that he became common. Scott, by catching the type at its very first appearance, envisages the future and throws it into dramatic contrast with Vich Ian Vohr, Fergus MacIvor, the belated representative of the past, artificially preserved in the special atmospheres of St. Germains and Glennaquoich.

Scott suggests, in *Waverley*, that the man of feeling, and the whole cult of 'sensibility', were originally English phenomena which could make no way in Scotland until older indigenous habits of thought and feeling were destroyed at Culloden, for Scottish Whig and Scottish Jacobite alike. If so, the Scots learnt fast. For the English prophets of the movement, Richardson and Sterne, had to be bowdlerized before they could fit the requirements of the cult; whereas by 1770 the Athens of the North was supplying London, through Mackenzie and Macpherson, Beattie and Logan, Boswell and (soon after) Burns, with all the literature characteristic of the new vogue. As late as 1814, it seems, this era appeared to the Scots a great cultural achievement on the part of their countrymen; and Scott's dedication shows that, despite all the affection he felt for an older Scotland, he too regarded Mackenzie, and all that he stood for, as something to be applauded.

Indeed, we must go further. Among those 'rarest and most valuable volumes' with which Edward Waverley was to garnish the library of Waverley Honour might we not expect to find *La Picara Justina Diez*—'which, by the way, is one of the most rare books of Spanish literature'? At any rate, the Sternian pen that 'can speedily change from grave to gay, and from description and dialogue to narrative and character' was never so much valued as by those who catered for the cult of 'sensibility'. Among the men of feeling we have to list the author of *Waverley* himself.

Whether Walter Scott and 'the author of *Waverley*' are at all points one and the same person is another matter. In view of the author's jealously guarded anonymity, it would be possible to argue that when Scott wrote *Waverley*, he was writing in an assumed character, as Sterne wrote in the character of Yorick. But at any rate, if we think that Scott was in some sort a 'man of feeling' himself, it throws light on his avowed object, 'to procure sympathy'. Of that aspect of Scott's intention and achievement (and by his own account it is the most important aspect), I have said nothing at all, because there is no way of saying it. I have, after all, considered *Waverley* as a work of discrimination and judgement, as if the whole book were written in the style of the first seven chapters. But it is written to procure our sympathies, and it is on that count that it stands or falls. Here every reader can only judge for himself whether his sympathies are engaged, and how strongly. For my own part I am moved continually and powerfully, and it is because I am so moved that I consider *Waverley* one of the greatest novels in the language. The most an essay of this kind can do is to show that if our sympathies are engaged, they are not engaged indiscriminately but to some purpose. That cannot be said of all Scott's books; but it can be said of this one.

IV

PAN TADEUSZ

ᘻᘻᘻᘻᘻᘻᘻᘻᘻᘻᘻᘻᘻᘻᘻᘻᘻᘻᘻᘻᘻᘻᘻᘻᘻᘻᘻᘻᘻ

Mᴵᶜᴷᴵᴱᵂᴵᶜᶻ's man of feeling is the young Count, who plays in *Pan Tadeusz* the fourth hand necessary to make up a double triangle with the hero and his two women, Zosia and Telimena. The Count has all the features of the type, down to the sketching pencil in the pocket and the taste for the Gothic in literature, architecture and manners. Mickiewicz treats him with an affectionate indulgence, making comedy out of his inability to distinguish between the ideally imagined and the actual; and it is this no doubt which leads the critics to call him Quixotic and invoke the name of Cervantes. All the same it does not strike me as a useful identification. Or rather, it is once again a case which is clarified by Scott's heraldic metaphor of 'the bearings' and 'the tincture'. The Quixotic is perhaps an undying recurrent type, and to this extent the bearings of Cervantes remain the same in Mickiewicz; but the tincture is unmistakeably that of the period, of the man of feeling. Scott appears to have no qualms about the man of feeling. But it was a type which had already deteriorated. By Byron's day the epicure of the feelings, continually probing his own emotions to induce new and more exotic feelings, was suffering already from a jaded palate, having enjoyed all the available tastes before he was past his youth, and therefore the prey of ennui and *le mal du siècle*. His later history is well known, and it was Russian authors who traced it most closely, from the Onegin of Pushkin through the Pechorin of Lermontov to the Stavrogin of Dostoievsky. Mickiewicz acknowledges these darker potentialities of the type only once, I think, when the Count realizes how his imagination has obscured the reality of the heroine, Zosia:

> His soul like the earth after sundown
> Darkened and chilled; his abstraction
> Brought him bad dreams; he awakened
> In anger that sought its occasion.

But in the poem as a whole Mickiewicz treats this figure with humorous indulgence, with none of Scott's sense that this type is the man of the future. And he is farther still from entertaining any of Pushkin's much darker forebodings about characters of this type.

In any case, however, *Waverley* is related to both *Pan Tadeusz* and *The Captain's Daughter* in a far more obvious way, by virtue of its unheroic hero. Mr. Czeslaw Milosz observes this in *Pan Tadeusz* when he says of Mickiewicz that 'The humour with which he sets his limited and mediocre heroes in motion is without malice'. My information doesn't extend so far as to know whether Polish critics earlier than Mr. Milosz have made heavier weather of this 'weakness' in Mickiewicz's Tadeusz. But the Russian critics have censured Pushkin for his 'limited and mediocre' Grinyov in just the same way as the English critics have objected to Scott's Edward Waverley. Belinsky, no less, writing in 1846 on *The Captain's Daughter*, decided 'The insignificant, colourless character of the hero of the story and his beloved Marya Ivanovna . . . belong to its striking shortcomings'. And we have to wait for Leontiev before finding it acknowledged that, as Professor Lednicki has said, 'the average character of the narrator' is 'the finest, the unique device of Pushkin the historian'. I wish to suggest that Scott had something to do with Pushkin's discovery of this 'device', as with Mickiewicz's discovery of it about the same time.

Thackeray, when he subtitled *Vanity Fair* 'a novel without a hero', meant by that something very interesting but quite different from what it may mean as applied to *Waverley*. The formula fits the Scott novel just as neatly. And the enormous advantage of the Scott method in this particular is that it makes of the central character a sounding-board for historical reverberations, or else, to change the metaphor, a weathervane responding to every shift in the winds of history which blow around it. This device, and this alone, of a weak hero poised and vacillating between opposites allows the historian to hold the balance absolutely firm and impartial, giving credit everywhere it is due. If the central figure is exempted from judgement, this is not from any moral laxity in the story-teller; but is designed to permit judgement of the parties, the ideologies, the alternative societies which contend for his allegiance. Thus, just as Scott's hero is poised between MacIvor and Talbot, between Scottish and English, between Jacobite and Hanoverian, between past and future, so Pushkin's Grinyov is poised between the peasant rebel and pretender Pugachov and the true Czar represented by his own father and the father of his sweetheart; and so Mickiewicz's Tadeusz is poised between Zosia and Telimena, between a healthy provincialism centred on Vilno and a superficially more sophisticated but really more damaging provincialism which looks to St. Petersburg.

According to Mr. David Daiches, this holding of the balance between phases of history is the true theme of all Scott's good novels, the true 'plot' to which what Mr. Daiches calls 'the external plot' is irrelevant. That this is the true theme I would agree. But I do not think that the question of Scott's plots can be dismissed quite so easily. For if the apparent plot bears no relation to the true theme, this is surely a major flaw in the writing. Yet this, or something like it, is the best that another of Scott's modern apologists, Mr. Edwin Muir, can do for him:

Scott was a very great story-teller, as well as a very bad one. *The Antiquary* certainly contains one of his worst plots. But his particular kind of story-telling did not depend on plot, and was often good in spite of it, the story being excellent even where the plot was mediocre or bad.[1]

This, I'm afraid, strikes me as playing with words. Of course, the whole notion of 'plot' in literature is one that has been in bad odour for a long time, ever since Henry James declared exultantly of a novel by Turgenev, 'And never a patch of plot, to draw blood!' And certainly, if the only questions to be asked of plot are 'Does it keep us wondering what is coming next?' and 'Is this the way things happen in daily life?'—if these are the only criteria to be applied to plot (and they are the only questions commonly asked), then indeed 'plot' is an irrelevance, a mere conventional machine. But lately we have begun to wonder again what Aristotle meant when he laid down the principle of unity of action in drama, and to wonder if this has not some bearing on questions of plot in narrative as well. If we follow this line of thought, we find ourselves deciding that a plot is no worse for being totally unlike what happens in daily life, as in the case of fairy-stories or *Oedipus Rex*; and none the worse either if we know throughout all that is coming next, as in the case of *Oedipus Rex* again. What is required is that, whatever the elaborations of the plot, all of these should be firmly related to a central action which is banally simple and a sort of symbolic pivot for the theme. As Mr. Daiches points out, Edward Waverley's proposal of marriage to Rose Brad-wardine rather than Flora MacIvor is just such a symbolic action, which justifies all the rest, and makes the plot of *Waverley* a very good one indeed. For where the central action is so firmly related to the theme, it can be embellished with sub-plots which, however fantastic and implausible in themselves, do not damage the form.

[1] Edwin Muir, *Essays on Literature and Society* (1944).

Considering plots in this way, we soon find ourselves thinking in terms of the twelve or thirty-two or however-many-it-is
'basic plots'. And from this it is only a step to the territory of
archetypes and depth-psychology, which is a landscape that I
must confess I don't much like the look of. But we may, and
indeed we must, penetrate a little way into this jungle. For
Waverley and *The Captain's Daughter* and *Pan Tadeusz* (to
which we may add another of Scott's best novels, *Redgauntlet*)
all make play with one of the hoariest of all archetypal plots,
the plot of the lost father, a situation which occurs rarely in
daily life but frequently in literature. In *Waverley* this fairy-
tale element is sketched in so lightly, and accommodated so
scrupulously to the demands of everyday likelihood, that it is
easily overlooked. But in fact Edward Waverley has a mildly
unnatural father, a time-serving politician, who is so intent on
making a career in London that he leaves his son to be brought
up in the family home by an uncle with Jacobite sympathies
and connections. Thus Waverley's involvement with the
Jacobites and his gradual extrication from them, throughout
the book, represent his search for the real father, the Hanoverian Whig, behind the figure of the substitute father, the
Tory uncle. And sure enough, it is the father's influence with
the prevailing party which finally procures Waverley a pardon.
Mickiewicz's Tadeusz is similarly brought up by an uncle, the
Judge, and discovers his true father only at the end of the story;
and, since the true father is an agitator on behalf of the advancing Napoleonic armies, he represents the future with which
Tadeusz allies himself when at the end he joins the army of
liberation. But it was a short future, for the Napoleonic liberation was short-lived; and so the end of *Pan Tadeusz*, a conclusion tragic in feeling after so much smilingly indulgent
comedy, is far more complex and affecting than anything in
Scott. And one is left with the impression that the false father,
the uncle, is ultimately the true father after all, in the sense that
he represents the innate strength of Lithuanian Poland, and

this is the only basis on which to build; whereas the true father has pinned his hopes on the French, who have betrayed the Poles hardly less than the Russians have.

In terms of artistic strategy, Mickiewicz is much the boldest of the three writers: by having the true father hover continually in disguise about the developing action, he risks the fairytale far more, and challenges daily plausibility far more defiantly than either Scott or Pushkin. Pushkin is by far the most deft and economical in his handling of the lost-father element. In keeping with the whole of *The Captain's Daughter*, a novel resolutely stripped of all superfluities, in which every word is made to count, this whole symbolic dimension of the story is opened up only once, in the dream that Grinyov has after his first meeting with Pugatchov, at a time when he still does not know who Pugatchov is. I must be permitted to quote this afresh:

> I had a dream which I could never since forget and in which I still see a kind of prophecy when I reflect upon the strange vicissitudes of my life. The reader will forgive me, probably knowing from experience how natural it is for man to indulge in superstition, however great his contempt for all vain imaginings may be.

He dreams that he returns to the home which he has lately left to join his regiment, and that his mother meets him, telling him his father is dying:

> Terror-stricken, I followed her to the bedroom. It was dimly lighted; people with sad-looking faces were standing by the bed. I approached the bed quietly; my mother lifted the bed-curtains and said: 'Andrey Petrovitch! Petrusha has come; he returned when he heard of your illness; bless him.' I knelt down and looked at the sick man. But what did I see? Instead of my father a black-bearded peasant lay on the bed looking at me merrily. I turned to my mother in perplexity, and said to her: 'What does it mean? This is not my father. And why should I ask this peasant's blessing?'—'Never mind, Petrusha,' my mother answered, 'he takes

your father's place for the wedding; kiss his hand and let him bless you. . . .' I would not do it. Then the peasant jumped off the bed, seized an axe from behind his back, and began waving it about. I wanted to run away and could not; the room was full of dead bodies; I stumbled against them and slipped in the pools of blood. . . . The terrible peasant called to me kindly, saying: 'Don't be afraid, come and let me bless you.' Terror and confusion possessed me . . . At that moment I woke up.

By the end of the book, when Grinyov has been helped to his bride by the peasant-pretender Pugatchov, when he has seen Pugatchov hang his friends before his eyes, when he has seen Pugatchov executed in his turn, there is hardly an item of this dream—not the wedding, the pools of blood, the obdurate 'I would not'—that lacks symbolic resonance, of the compelling sort that continually asks to be reduced to allegory but in the end always escapes that reduction. And meanwhile verisimilitude is scrupulously preserved. For this is what dreams are like; the characteristically Dostoievskyan vertigo which comes of a forcing together of incompatible feelings is from this point of view very exactly, almost clinically, 'realistic'. And the more one looks at this passage, the harder it is to deny to the Soviet critics at least part of their case that Pushkin, writing under immediate personal censorship from the Czar, yet contrived by sheerly artistic means to express rabidly subversive sentiments.

Now, one must guard against the ludicrous idea (which, ludicrous as it is, is not uncommon) that the writer has only to tap the archetype, which will thereupon write his masterpiece for him. The lost-father archetype is of no artistic value whatever, until it is placed in a context in which its symbolic overtones are meaningful, in which the search for the father can become the search for the birthright, for the source of true authority to which allegiance can rightfully be given. The archetype is profitable for Scott, for Mickiewicz, for Pushkin, only because all three authors have established the ranges of choice that are open, the different allegiances which present themselves in all their baffling incompatible plausibility at a given moment of history. And meanwhile we may note that the hero in the lost-father fable *has to be* what Scott and the others have made him—wavering (there is a sort of pun with 'Waverley'), inconstant, mediocre, weak. How else should he behave, since, not knowing his father, he does not know who he is, nor where his allegiance lies?

There is another basic plot or archetypal fable in *Waverley* and in *Pan Tadeusz*—what may be called the Romeo-and-Juliet plot, of the youth and the maiden born to warring houses, who fall in love with each other. This does not occur in *The Captain's Daughter*, though it is the basic fable of Pushkin's earlier and unfinished novel *Dubrovsky*. It is also the basic fable of *The Bride of Lammermoor*, and accordingly critics have found in that novel by Scott the source or one source for Pushkin's story. This attribution does not recommend itself to me, for these basic fables are by definition widely available, and nothing else in *Dubrovsky* reminds me of *The Bride of Lammermoor*. What is more interesting than anything else which emerges from these comparisons is the striking contrast between Pushkin and Mickiewicz in their procedures. Pushkin's abstemiousness—his allocation of one fable to one story—is in line with his constant practice in all kinds of writing, his classical severity, his concern above all to have only one line of interest and action running clean and unfettered. I am not so sure whether it is typical of Mickiewicz to do the other thing, though I think it is. As to *Pan Tadeusz*, there can be no doubt: where Pushkin strips his story to the bone, Mickiewicz accumulates and elaborates. The lost-father theme at its most challengingly implausible is pointed up by Mickiewicz and brought out of the discreet shadow where Scott had left it; the Romeo-and-Juliet plot is planted firmly on top of it; not content with the triangle situation which thereupon emerges, Mickiewicz introduces a fourth young man to make a double triangle; the Lithuanian Montagues and Capulets are brought face to face in a pitched battle; and below and behind these numerous actions, all in some degree private, surges always the public drama of the Napoleonic invasion of Russia. And no one of these lines of action is allowed to run so smoothly that it cannot loiter into digressions, lyrical invocations, set-pieces of genre-painting, vignettes from a comedy of manners. If Pushkin's manner is classical, Mickiewicz's is exuberantly Gothic; and if *Pan Tadeusz* is a novel-in-verse, then *The Captain's Daughter* is a poem in prose. For this is the astonishing thing; we are accustomed to allow that prose is more cumulative in effect than poetry, and so to allow to prose far more liberty to elaborate and discursively accumulate than we allow to poetry. Yet in this case it is the poem, Mickiewicz's, which is leisurely, digressive, cumulative, and the novel, Pushkin's, which has all the severity and rapidity.

It is our conviction or prejudice about the simplicity of plot in poetry which makes us suspicious of the whole genre of the novel-in-verse. In any case, we have in English no generally acknowledged masterpieces in this kind. The nearest we can come to it in modern times is Byron's *Don Juan* or Wordsworth's *Excursion* (and of course it is no accident that both these works belong to the Romantic period, as does *Pan Tadeusz*), but everyone will admit that in the end these poems are something else again; and so we are left with Mrs. Browning's *Aurora Leigh* as the best example of a genre which that curious work has not served to make respectable among us. Confessing so much, we are often asked to relate *Pan Tadeusz* to an accepted masterpiece in this kind, Pushkin's *Eugene Onegin*. But in fact this is worse than useless, for in that work, despite the digressions and vignettes which remind us of *Pan Tadeusz* as of Byron's *Don Juan*, Pushkin's narrative leanness is carried to a splendid extreme. For the plot can be reduced, as Professor Lednicki has said, to the formula: A loves B, but B does not love A; B falls in love with A when A can no longer

love B. In the massive simplicity of this there is nothing that
can lull our disquiets about the complexities of plot in *Pan
Tadeusz*. And indeed I do not know how to lull them, except
by pointing out that they immediately go to sleep of themselves
as soon as we begin to read. And this means, I think, that we
accept the elaboration of the action because it is all of a piece
with everything else. It is not that the plot is elaborated at the
expense of anything else. On the contrary, the same exuberant
inventiveness which is continually throwing out new complica-
tions in the story is at the same time inexhaustibly devouring
the commonplace, elevating and idealizing it at every turn with
apt and beautiful metaphor. And if Mickiewicz falls foul of our
preconceptions about the simplicity of plot proper to poetry,
he falls in with a set of preconceptions far less ancient but far
more powerful—our admiration for the particular and the
concrete in poetry, especially when these go along with creative
metaphor. An example is his evocation of the Lithuanian sky:

> Blue, that Italian sky
> Clear, as is frozen water;
> But in this country
> As the wind or the storm passes,
> What images, what actions
> The sportive wrack composes:
> Shower-logged, sluggish in Spring
> Clouds like tortoises labour
> Over a sky where tresses
> Of the long rain sway earthward;
> The bowling hailstorm crosses
> The heavens by balloon
> Blue, but with yellow flashes;
> And then, what metamorphoses
> Pursue the white quotidian
> Clouds that like a gaggle
> Of swans or geese the falcon
> Wind hard presses;
> Harried, they multiply

48

Prodigies, and crested
With sudden manes as serried
Legs bud beneath them, coursers
Over the steppes of the sky,
Necks arched, they gallop.

This stream of images, clouds in wind becoming tortoises, locks of hair, balloons, swans and geese and falcons, and galloping horses—all in rapid succession as if by cutting in the cinema—this is the sort of thing we are very ready to admire. After all, it is the Shakespearean thing; and we respond to it very readily, far more readily (it is worth pointing out) than to anything in Pushkin, whose imagination works in a quite different and far less translatable way. Moreover, there is one very important element in *Pan Tadeusz*—an element rather of character than plot—which is treated throughout in the poet's way, not the novelist's way. This is the figure of the heroine Zosia, the unformed and vulnerable Juliet to the Romeo of the young Tadeusz. Zosia is on the stage far less than her thematic importance would seem to require. When she *is* on stage, she is hardly ever in the centre of it, but a fugitive apparition glimpsed obliquely and entrancingly as she disappears into the wings. And even a translation can reveal that if this figure none the less pulls its weight, it is because of the *quality* which inheres in her brief appearances, a quality of intensity in language which I think we have to call lyrical, and a quality which *by* its intensity, counterbalances the far more cumulative, particularized and even analytical treatment given to her more mature rival, her aunt Telimena. If we compare this treatment of Zosia with Pushkin's treatment of a similar figure, Tatiana in *Eugene Onegin*, I think we have to say that in this particular it is Pushkin who is more the novelist-in-verse, Mickiewicz who is more the poet. This is the point at which to acknowledge that of course there *is* a novel-in-verse in English which is an acknowledged masterpiece, Chaucer's *Troilus and Criseyde*. Criseyde is treated with the novelist's hand as much as

Pushkin's Tatiana is, or Mickiewicz's Telimena. And I should be happy if someone would draw the conclusion that such terms as I have been using, singleness of action, are still or may be as relevant to the discussion of poems as of novels and dramas—as of course they were always supposed to be by neo-classical critics.

Yet to give the flavour of Mickiewicz's incomparable poem to those who do not know it, one needs to point, not to a piece of static description, but to what is far more remarkable, the sustained passages describing tumultuous and fluctuating action. And more remarkable than either are the gradations and transitions of tone as of matter by which the poet slides in and out of his digressions and his set-pieces. It was precisely this feature of Pushkin's *Eugene Onegin* which Mickiewicz drew attention to when he lectured on the poem in Paris, remarking that 'the reader does not even notice how from the key of an ode the poem descends to an epigram and, rising again, passes imperceptibly into a fragment told with almost epic gravity.'[1]

It need not be pretended that these aspects of Mickiewicz's art can be paralleled in Walter Scott, or that they have any relation to what Mickiewicz may have learned from Scott—beyond this: that *Pan Tadeusz* can carry the weight of inventiveness at the level of diction as at the level of plot, only because the plot, for all its elaboration, is at bottom, as the neo-classic theorists used to say, *a single action*, and a single action on the model of Scott's central action in *Waverley*, made symbolic and central by just the means that Scott employed there and elsewhere. And so it is no surprise that Mickiewicz himself, even as he wrote *Pan Tadeusz*, described the poem as nearest in genre to a Scott novel.[2]

To turn to Pushkin is to enter a world in human terms very similar but utterly different in terms of artistic strategies.

[1] Quoted by Waclaw Lednicki, *Bits of Table Talk on Pushkin, Mickiewicz, Goethe, Turgenev and Sienkiewicz* (The Hague, 1956), p. 24.

[2] Weintraub, *The Poetry of Adam Mickiewicz*, p. 223.

Pushkin's novels and short stories, except perhaps for the *Queen of Spades*, reveal their narrative structures with unparalleled nakedness. And just for that reason one feels that *The Captain's Daughter* is hardly a novel at all, just as Pushkin's stories are hardly stories. *The Captain's Daughter* is like the Platonic idea of the perfect novel; it is the idea, the incomparable symmetry and economy in the fitting of means to ends, which remain with us from the reading and which we suppose, perhaps unfairly, is what most interested the novelist in the writing. By the same token it is the bare hard impersonality of style, its inexorable movement from subject through verb to object, which is truly poetic prose—not the yearning cadences and jewelled imagery of the prose of W. B. Yeats, but everything sacrificed to concentration and rapidity. I fall among paradoxes. But this at least must be said: that Pushkin in prose is a virtuoso, interested above all in the technical problems of a strange and new medium. (For Russian narrative prose in any serviceable mode was all to make when Pushkin began writing; and Pushkin duly made it, for himself and for others.) This virtuosity reaches its peak in Pushkin's short stories, the *Tales of Belkin*, but the same brilliance is apparent in only slightly less degree in *The Captain's Daughter*. I have already remarked on the singleness of the symbolic action in the novel, a principle learned I suspect from Scott, but here applied with a rigour quite alien to Scott's temper of mind; and this is the central and most important case of virtuosity in the work. But I will remark briefly on two others, devices which once again Pushkin may have found in Scott, but only in a rudimentary form. I mean the device of the framed narrator, and the device of the epigraph.

Pushkin's early unfinished novels, *Dubrovsky* and *The Negro of Peter the Great* are both written *in propria persona*: that is to say, the voice that we hear telling the tale is that of the omniscient narrator, quite uninvolved in the action he recounts. But in *The Captain's Daughter* as also in the *Tales of Belkin* the man who tells the story is himself part of the story, and we see it all through the none too perceptive or clear-sighted eyes of Grinyov in one case, Belkin in the other. Scott, in novels later than *Waverley*, had made perfunctory gestures in this direction, grouping his stories as 'Tales of my Landlord', and sometimes placing between the reader and the story the shadowy figure of an imaginary narrator, Jedediah Cleishbotham; but Scott never made anything of the device, and indeed, most of the time in *The Heart of Midlothian*, for instance, we forget about Cleishbotham altogether as I'm sure Scott did too.[1] But this one simple device of the framed narrator, as developed particularly by Turgenev, was handed on by Turgenev to James, and thence to Joseph Conrad and Ford Madox Ford, issuing at last in the elaborations of the Henry James prefaces, with their theory of 'the limited point of view', in the intricacies of Conrad's *Chance*, where the framed narrator reconstructs a scene described to him by another character who herself has only a report of it from yet another, and in the tour-de-force of Ford's *The Good Soldier*. It is hardly too much to say that the whole cycle of this development was foreseen and followed through by Pushkin in the capsulated form of the *Tales of Belkin*, as in a sort of controlled experiment.

Once the novelist agrees to tell a story through the limited sensibility of a framed narrator, his problem of course is how to transcend these self-sought limitations in order to light up the narrative from an angle that the fictitious narrator cannot perceive. Turgenev and James, Conrad and Ford, all had their own ways of getting round this difficulty. Pushkin's device to

---

[1] Mickiewicz used something like this device in *Gra*ż*yna* but not I think in *Pan Tadeus*ż; though Professor Weintraub claims that there too the voice which tells the story is not that of the poet but of a framed narrator, a sort of village gossip. This view has been challenged, and in any case it seems that if there is a framed narrator in *Pan Tadeus*ż, he is present only vestigially.

this end was another one which he could have found in Scott; I mean, the epigraph. Scott's use of this device is already quite sophisticated, in such a case for instance as the epigraphs from Massinger's *New Way to Pay Old Debts* at the head of chapters in *The Bride of Lammermoor*. But here again Pushkin carried the device to an extreme of ingenuity; if one is to believe the brilliant Soviet scholar Viktor Shklovsky, Pushkin's epigraphs to the chapters of *The Captain's Daughter* carry, as it were in code, a reading of history directly opposed to the blamelessly conservative sentiments overtly professed by the narrator Grinyov.

Whatever we may think of Shklovsky's ingenious thesis as a whole, there is at least enough truth in it to make me guard against the impression I may have given, by my talk of 'virtuosity', that Pushkin was not intimately interested in the *subject* of *The Captain's Daughter*. He was of course avidly interested, and personally involved. The easiest way to establish this is to read, along with *The Captain's Daughter*, the unfinished *Negro of Peter the Great*, which is an exception to all I have said, in that it shows no sign of virtuosity but is the torso of a novel straightforwardly on Scott's plan and designed on a massive scale. There could have been no classic severity of outline here. In the few chapters which are completed we can see pre-Petrine Russia aligned against the Russia of Peter the Great, a closed Russia against a Russia open to the West, and a Russia administered by the traditional classes of the boyars and minor gentry against a Russia administered by a specially created cadre of bureaucrats, many of them foreigners. With a patriarchal boyar household on the one hand (and a heroine springing from it), and with on the other no less than three foreigners, the negro himself, a Swedish prisoner-of-war, and a Frenchified young aristocrat appalled by the Czar's bourgeois and Germanic entourage, the tapestry already has as many threads as Scott at his most ambitious would hardly try to weave together; and there is, over and above this, since the basic fable is the Romeo-and-Juliet one, a distracting and irrelevant question of the colour-bar. Altogether there was every reason why Pushkin abandoned the story, fascinating as it is so far as it goes. But when we read this fragment, and when we recall also that Pushkin was descended on his mother's side from in fact a negro favourite of Peter's, and on his father's side from precisely one of the gentle families whose hereditary functions had been usurped by these foreign favourites and paid administrators, we realize that the issue in *The Captain's Daughter* is not at all between Czarist autocracy on the one side and peasant democracy on the other. On the contrary, the conflict is between a patriarchal society on the one hand, and on the other an antagonist present only in innuendo and epigraph and the ambiguous figure of the German-Russian general Andrey Karlovich, that is to say, the Czarist bureaucracy. In short, Shklovsky is certainly so far right that there is more in this story than meets the eye; and though Pugatchov certainly stands for a way of life (heroic and barbarian like Scott's Vich Ian Vohr), so far as he is a peasant Pugatchov poses the question only whether the peasants fare better under the unjust patriarchal rule of the hereditary gentry, or under a remote autocracy operating through bureaucrats with no stake in the country and no organic ties with the peasants under them.

And so we come round once again to 'the solemn fraternity which a great nation composes—gathered together, in a stormy season, under the shade of ancestral feeling'. It appears when one has decoded the signals of the epigraphs to the chapters, that this is not just one of many feelings inspired by *The Captain's Daughter* and inspiring it, but the single strain of feeling which governs the whole. The same may be said of *Pan Tadeusz*, more certainly and more emphatically. For Mickiewicz's poem, celebrating the awakening of the Lithuanian nation to its nationhood and the chance of vindicating it, may be said to be presenting, in one massive and internally

complicated image, just what Wordsworth is talking about—
'the power of injustice and inordinate calamity to transmute,
to invigorate, and to govern—to sweep away the barriers of
opinion—to reduce under submission passions purely evil—
to exalt the nature of indifferent qualities, and to render them
fit companions for the absolute virtues with which they are
summoned to associate—to consecrate passions which, if
not bad in themselves, are of such temper that, in the calm of
ordinary life, they are rightly deemed so—to correct and embody these passions—and, without weakening them (nay, with
tenfold addition to their strength), to make them worthy of
taking their place as the advanced guard of hope, when a
sublime movement of deliverance is to be originated; . . .'
The same necessity which produces Wordsworth's intricately
exciting and accumulative syntax produces in Mickiewicz's
poem the wealth of digression, illustration, and incident; and
the catalogues of minutiae like the listing of the varieties of
mushrooms. What operates in both writers and determines
their procedures is the same conviction of how natural laws of
communal feeling operate surely yet with unmasterable subtlety of ramification and cross-reference. It is for this reason
that a novel—or at least a novel with this theme—has to be,
in the word of Ortega y Gasset, 'sluggish', has to proceed at
a snail's pace, by accumulating minutiae. Only in this way can
justice be done to the weavings and interweavings and mutual
transmutations by which a community becomes and remains
more than the sum of the individuals which compose it. And
it is for this reason that, however grateful we may be for
Pushkin's terseness and elegance, yet what he does in *The
Captain's Daughter* is somehow eccentric, is not what the novel
is by its very nature. And it is for this reason that *Pan Tadeusz*,
though a poem, is more of a novel or else a better novel than
The Captain's Daughter is.

V

ROB ROY

꧁꧂꧁꧂꧁꧂꧁꧂꧁꧂꧁꧂꧁꧂꧁꧂꧁꧂꧁꧂꧁꧂꧁꧂꧁꧂꧁꧂

'ROB ROY', written four years after the appearance of *Waverley*, challenges comparison with that masterpiece and comes badly out of the comparison.

The question at issue in the book seems, at least as far as half-way, to be much the same as that in *Waverley*. It is neatly focussed in a conversation between Frank Osbaldistone and Diana Vernon, about the portrait of one of her ancestors:

'Pipes!—they look more like penny-whistles. But, pray, do not be angry with my ignorance,' I continued, observing the colour mount to her cheeks, 'I can mean no affront to your armorial bearings, for I do not even know my own.'

'You an Osbaldistone, and confess so much!' she exclaimed. 'Why, Percie, Thornie, John, Dickon—Wilfred himself, might be your instructor. Even ignorance itself is a plummet over you.'

'With shame I confess it, my dear Miss Vernon, the mysteries couched under the grim hieroglyphics of heraldry are to me as unintelligible as those of the pyramids of Egypt.'

'What! is it possible? Why, even my uncle reads Gwillym sometimes of a winter night. Not know the figures of heraldry? —of what could your father be thinking?'

'Of the figures of arithmetic,' I answered; 'the most insignificant unit of which he holds more highly than all the blazonry of chivalry. But, though I am ignorant to this inexpressible degree, I have knowledge and taste enough to admire that splendid picture, in which I think I can discover a family likeness to you.

56

What ease and dignity in the attitude—what richness of colouring—what breadth and depth of shade!'

'Is it really a fine painting?' she asked.

'I have seen many works of the renowned artist,' I replied,
'but never beheld one more to my liking.'

'Well, I know as little of pictures as you do of heraldry,'
replied Miss Vernon; 'yet I have the advantage of you, because
I have always admired the painting without understanding its
value.'

Unfortunately the implications of this difference of opinion
are never thoroughly worked out. And it is an important
matter, being not just a difference of opinion but a difference
about moral standards. Miss Vernon holds by the principle
of honour, Osbaldistone (or rather not he, but the party he at
this point represents—pre-eminently his father) stand by the
principle of *credit*.

'Upon all these matters I am now to ask your advice, Mr.
Jarvie, which, I have no doubt, will point out the best way to act
for my father's advantage and my own honour.'

'Ye're right, young man—ye're right,' said the Bailie. 'Aye
take the counsel of those who are aulder and wiser than yoursell,
and binna like the godless Rehoboam, who took the advice o'
a wheen beardless callants, neglecting the old counsellors who
had sat at the feet o' his father Solomon, and, as it was weel put
by Mr. Meiklejohn, in his lecture on the chapter, were doubtless partakers of his sapience. But I maun hear naething about
honour—we ken naething here but about credit. Honour is
a homicide and a bloodspiller, that gangs about making frays in
the street; but Credit is a decent honest man, that sits at hame and
makes the pat play.'

It is sometimes said (John Buchan says it) that the book
takes as it were an unconscionable time to get airborne, and
that it comes to life only when Osbaldistone crosses the Scottish border. And it cannot be denied that there is a distinct
and welcome quickening of the narrative pace at this point,

and that this acceleration is thereafter maintained. On the other hand, it is important to recognize that the earlier situations have been very well contrived to bring out the significance of that conflict of standards which I have tried to isolate above. For instance old Osbaldistone's rejection of his patrimony, the ancestral estates (and Scott goes out of his way to emphasize that whereas this may have been forced on the old merchant in the first place, he has since embraced it as a policy—deliberately cut loose), takes on, in the light of what old Osbaldistone seems to stand for, a symbolic significance. In fact we should not be so dissatisfied with the early chapters if the title alone—let alone Scott's introductory matter on sources—had not prepared us for something quite different. These chapters are a very good introduction to a novel, but not to the novel we have been led to expect, a 'high romance'. The crossing of the border is the crucial point where the story completely changes its direction and its tone. And so we can regard it *either* as a romance spoiled by a cumbrous initial development *or* as a realistic novel spoiled by a second half which turns out to be romance. Take it either way and we are compelled—so far as I can see—to put it down a failure.

Why did Scott thus change horses in mid-stream? All sorts of answers could be given, but there is one element in the novel up to the crossing of the border which made some such expedient inevitable if the story was to be salvaged even in part. This is the character of the supposed hero and narrator, Frank Osbaldistone himself. Many readers have found him weak and colourless; but then the same is said of Edward Waverley. There is, however, all the difference in the world. For Scott's presentation of Waverley is a strong portrait of a weak or weakish character; his treatment of Osbaldistone is a weak portrait. In the one case the weakness is in the character, not in the creation, which is masterly; with Osbaldistone the weakness is all in the presentation. Waverley's vacillations are essential to the role he has to play, they are convincingly motivated, and they are presented quite clearly yet without alienating the reader's sympathies. More important still, Waverley's weakness is historically plausible—he stands for something, is a type of the embryonic man of feeling, the proto-Romantic, whose appearance on the scene *c.* 1745 is historically correct and in keeping. By pushing the period thirty years farther back, to 1715 instead of 1745, Scott denied himself the chance of drawing on this historically verifiable change of spirit, in order to motivate his central figure. Osbaldistone, in so far as he emerges at all, is an anachronism. The man of feeling had not emerged by 1715, and Osbaldistone's response to Highland scenery, no less than his aversion to commerce, are not only not accounted for—the balance of historical probability is against them. Osbaldistone has just enough life to qualify as a hero of romance. of whom all that is asked is that he should be young, guileless and brave; he is quite inadequate as the hero of the sort of book Scott found himself writing, an analysis, in historically realistic terms, of the state of English society in the first half of the eighteenth century. Hence, we may argue, Scott *had* to turn his novel into a romance half way through, just because he had furnished himself with a hero who was fit for nothing else.

Another consequence of putting the clock farther back (to 1715 instead of 1745) is that it purged Scott's vision of the nostalgia with which he viewed the later Jacobite period in *Waverley*. Nostalgia is strong in *Waverley*, though thoroughly under control. From *Rob Roy* it is completely absent. And this could have been a very good thing. It qualified Scott to attempt what, in the figures of Rob Roy and his wife, he in some measure achieved—that is, the bleakly heroic effect. But the purging of nostalgia had less welcome and rather surprising effects.

In *Waverley* Scott attempts to strike a balance between the old order and the new in the middle of the eighteenth century. Between his nostalgia for the old and his complacency in the new, the balance is beautifully maintained; and the vacillations of Waverley, the central figure, are the very happy dramatic symbol of this. In *Rob Roy* Scott tries again to strike a balance between old and new, but at an earlier point in history; and because this earlier period is more remote (Scott could have known men who fought at Culloden, but none who fought at Prestonpans), the nostalgia disappears and there is nothing left to counterbalance the complacency. The commercial order represented in England by Osbaldistone the father, and in Scotland by Nicol Jarvie, is, as Scott recognized, the foundation of his own Regency order of society about which he was well-satisfied. For instance, the Osbaldistone clerk Owen is made to speak in terms of the moral accountancy that in Scott's own day had developed into the attitudes of Benthamism:

> 'Mr. Francis,' said the head clerk, with his usual formal inclination of the head, and a slight elevation of his right hand, which he had acquired by a habit of sticking his pen behind his ear before he spoke—'Mr. Francis seems to understand the fundamental principle of all moral accounting, the great ethic rule of three. Let A do to B, as he would have B do to him; the product will give the rule of conduct required.'
> My father smiled at this reduction of the golden rule to arithmetical form, but instantly proceeded.

To be sure, Scott makes fun of this, but very indulgently.

At any rate, in striking contrast to the nostalgia for the old order in *Waverley*, in *Rob Roy* Scott so much admires the new order that the old gets less than justice. This is certainly true of Sir Hildebrand Osbaldistone and his sons. Sir Hildebrand stands for Old England just as the Baron Bradwardine in *Waverley* stood for Old Scotland:

> 'Ay, true, Die,—true,' said Sir Hildebrand, with a sigh. 'I misdoubt Rashleigh will be found short at the leap when he is put to the trial. An he would ha' learned useful knowledge like

his brothers, he was bred up where it grew, I wuss; but French antics, and book-learning, with the new turnips, and the rats, and the Hanoverians, ha' changed the world that I ha' known in old England.'

Sir Hildebrand's sentiments are those of the verses that Fielding wrote to 'The Roast Beef of Old England'. The Baron Brad-wardine in *Waverley* makes just such elegiac conversation, at greater length and more eloquently. That, it is plain, we are meant to take largely at face-value; whereas we are allowed to be under no illusions about Sir Hildebrand, having already seen the allegedly 'useful' knowledge of Rashleigh's brutish, sullen and debauched brothers. Scott's picture of Sir Hildebrand and his household is savagely contemptuous. And he goes too far when he allows Justice Inglewood to say that Sir Hildebrand, having lost one of his sons, was often at a loss to know which one it was. This is a joke, perhaps; but a joke in bad taste, surely. So much, at any rate, for Old England; the most that Scott can say for her is in the perfunctory comment on Fair-service's homestead at Osbaldistone Hall, which 'announced the warm and cordial comforts which Old England, even at her most northern extremity, extends to her meanest inhabi-tants'. Moreover, if we are to take the MacGregors as a special case (and Scott seems to want us to do so), then Old Scotland is represented by Garschattachin and the other Jacobite leaders in the clachan at Aberfoil; and they are treated with much the same sort of hard contempt—so that Old Scotland comes out of the examination hardly better than Old England.

Bailie Nicol Jarvie belongs to the second half of the book, which I have labelled 'romance'. Yet it could be maintained that in him we have the most elaborate piece of full-length 'realistic' presentation in the whole work. This is certainly true. But it is also true that Jarvie bursts out of his frame; and where-as some critics seem to take this as the highest praise, I mean by it rather to deplore once again Scott's slipshod method, his lack of concern for the internal economy of his composition.

Scott's presentation of Jarvie is 'realistic' as some of Dickens's presentations are realistic; he belongs in some unwritten novel as loose, exuberant and intricate as *Martin Chuzzlewit*. He is out of place in the Romantic second half of *Rob Roy*, and he would also be out of place in the first half, which is realistic certainly, but still in a way that makes no provision for Dickensian exuberance.

At one point, for instance, it seems as if Jarvie is to find his place in the book as a Scottish counterpart to old Osbaldistone; as a parallel case but also a variation on the type. Scott insists repeatedly that old Osbaldistone is a Romantic, he is in trade, not for what he can get out of it, but for the devil of it. He likes taking commercial risks. This, which can be regarded as Scott's interpretation of Addison's figure, Sir Andrew Freeport, is a genuine contribution to the understanding of history, to the drawing of a distinction between capitalism in its first expansive and adventurous phase, and the capitalism of a later age that is above all prudent and cautious. Moreover it bears upon what is perhaps the most important question of all for Scott: is human nature in all ages the same at bottom under different guises (the Romantic, for instance, perhaps a perennial type, appearing here in the role of commercial speculator); or does history throw up genuinely novel, unprecedented types? Jarvie at one point seems to be set over against Osbaldistone *père* as a quite different type with a different attitude to the commercial world—canny where Osbaldistone is intrepid:

> 'Mr. Osbaldistone is a gude honest gentleman; but I aye said he was ane o' them wad make a spune or spoil a horn, as my father the worthy deacon used to say. The deacon used to say to me, "Nick—young Nick . . . never put out your arm farther than ye can draw it easily back again." I hae said sae to Mr. Osbaldistone, and he didna seem to take it a'thegither sae kind as I wished—but it was weel meant—weel meant.'

It could be argued that caution was no more characteristic of

Scottish commerce than of English, in the period of the famous
John Law; yet Scott might plausibly have replied that Law was
an exception, and that 'canniness' was a strain in Scottish
temperament of whatever age. However, the contrast between
Osbaldistone and Jarvie is not maintained. Jarvie in fact takes
the considerable risk of going bail for Owen, and the Bailie
spreads himself over the later chapters to a degree quite out of
proportion with his place in—not the plot, but the symbolic
pattern behind the plot. In fact the composition has got so out
of hand that no such pattern emerges, and when we talk of it
we are talking in terms of what might have been.

We are sometimes asked to applaud the vitality of the figures
of Jarvie and Andrew Fairservice, and to contrast this with the
woodenness of the villain, Rashleigh, of the heroine, Diana
Vernon, and indeed of the hero, Frank. But this is to beg an
important question. Vitality, yes—but to what purpose?
The trouble with Nicol Jarvie is that this figure has altogether
too much vitality for the good of the book as a whole. And if
this is true of Jarvie, it is still more true of Fairservice, who is
nothing more than one huge excrescence on the story. He has
no part to play in the logic of the theme, so far as this can be
discerned. Those critics who choose to applaud him, like those
who make too much play with Savelyich in *The Captain's
Daughter*, see the novel-form as no more than a gallery of
colourful and verisimilar 'characters', a form to which the
matters of theme, action or 'plot' are irrelevant. It is true that
to deal thus ruthlessly is to treat Scott as if he were Henry
James. Scott, it is quite obvious, never dreamed of 'composition' in fiction, in the way James uses it, as analogous to composition in painting. And there is a school of literary historians
who would maintain that we have therefore no right to judge
Scott's novels by Jamesian criteria. But if we have read James or
Conrad or Ford, then when we read Scott inevitably we shall
measure him up against these others, just as we measure them
against him. And if *Rob Roy* cannot survive the comparison,

it is not the passage of time that is to blame; for *Waverley* stands up to it well enough.

It is worth insisting on this, for it is too often supposed that if we justify Edward Waverley, we have to justify Francis Osbaldistone also:

'To censure Scott for the woodenness of his heroes—characters like Edward Waverley, Francis Osbaldistone, and many others—is to misunderstand their function. They are not heroes in the ordinary sense, but symbolic observers. Their love affairs are of no significance whatsoever except to indicate the nature of the observer's final withdrawal from the seductive scenes of heroic, nationalist passion. Waverley does not marry the passionate Jacobite Flora MacIvor but the douce and colourless Rose Bradwardine; Waverley's affair with these two girls is not presented as a serious love interest, but as a symbolic indication of the nature of his final withdrawal from the heroic emotions of the past.'[1]

I think it is an overstatement to say that Waverley and Osbaldistone are 'observers'—both of them are far more involved in the action than that would suggest. But what is more important is to assert that it does damage to *Waverley* to have it linked, as here and as so often, with *Rob Roy*. In the one case the vacillation is all in the character portrayed; in the other, it is in the portrayal. It is the more important to make this point in that Mr. Daiches has of course got to the heart of the matter when he points out that Waverley's entanglement with the two Scottish girls is 'a symbolic indication' of something far more interesting. In Scotland when Scott wrote, no question was so vital as that of the possibility of 'marrying' two cultural traditions—the one barbarous and heroic, the other Hanoverian. When Waverley chooses to marry Rose Bradwardine he acts out Scott's answer to this question. The relations between Frank Osbaldistone and Diana Vernon continually promise some such symbolic meaning, but the promise is never redeemed.

[1] David Daiches, *Literary Essays*.

VI

MARIA EDGEWORTH

AT the end of *Castle Rackrent*, 'the Editor' (that is to say, Miss Edgeworth herself) declares that she 'lays it before the English reader as a specimen of manners and characters which are perhaps unknown in England'. This was to be echoed time and again throughout the nineteenth century by Irish writers, and this does them no good with Irish critics of the present day, who object reasonably enough that a sound national literature is addressed to the nation it professes to deal with; the author should be making his countrymen see themselves for what they are, not making foreigners regard them more indulgently. If we take Scott at his word, he is open to the same objection; as the Irish novelists realized when they all of them—Lever and Carleton and the Banim brothers and Lefanu—appealed to his precedent. His was a broader cloak for them to shelter under than the authority of their own compatriot, Miss Edgeworth. Yet when Scott himself had needed a precedent, he acknowledged that he had found it in her.

Since our sense of the greatness of *Waverley* requires us to see in it far more than what Scott gives as his avowed intention in the book, his acknowledgement to Miss Edgeworth might be taken as no more than a graceful compliment, were it not that in *Castle Rackrent* the Irish novelist too can be seen to have gone beyond her brief, and in a way very similar to Scott. For if we compare *Castle Rackrent* with *Waverley*, we see that Miss Edgeworth's pathetic hero, Sir Condy, is a historical as well as a national type; like the Baron Bradwardine in Scott's novel, he is the man who lives by the barbaric standard of honour in a commercial society where that standard can no longer apply. In the perspective of history, it could be argued, the Act of Union signified for Ireland what the failure of the Jacobites fifty years earlier had signified for Scotland, the final extinction of the code of honour as a standard of social conduct. Scott of course is fully aware of this historical perspective and establishes it with masterly precision without once stating it explicitly. It is implicit in *Castle Rackrent*, but in an altogether more shadowy way. That Miss Edgeworth was half-aware of the historical implications is revealed, I think, by her casting the whole into the mouth of Thady, the old retainer; for this gives to the story the elegiac tone of one who regrets or at any rate acknowledges the death of an old order, the irrelevance of much of his past.

The story also recalls (as Scott's, of course, doesn't) Goldsmith's *Vicar of Wakefield*. Sir Condy is like Goldsmith's Dr. Primrose and Dickens's Pickwick and even Dostoievsky's Idiot, in being the simpleton superior to and defeated by the society in which he moves. But Miss Edgeworth differs from Goldsmith and Dickens in refusing to idealize her simpleton. The unhappy ending is no accident; it goes along with, for instance, Sir Condy's sentimentality when he shams dead in order to hear the good that will be said of him at his wake. This is not just simple, but weak—Sir Condy is a weak character, for all his many virtues, and his creator does not shirk the fact. It is notable in this connection that when in fact Sir Condy does die, he is not much mourned for; if Thady is a faithful retainer, Judy M'Quirk for instance is not. His tenants have warm hearts (they rally to Sir Condy at first) but short memories. Sir Condy in fact recalls far more Goldsmith himself, so far as we know him, than he does Goldsmith's 'Vicar'.

It is this realism that makes *Castle Rackrent* so poetic—and that will seem a paradox only to those who have a false idea of poetry. For this reason it recalls, more clearly than either Goldsmith or Scott, another writer who declared himself indebted to Miss Edgeworth, Turgenev. Turgenev too uses the device of the fictional narrator, the tale-teller within the tale; Turgenev writes stories of the same scope and compass as *Castle Rackrent*, that is to say, *nouvelles* rather than novels; and in Turgenev is to be found the same union of poetry, usually elegiac poetry, and realism.

Yet the comparison with Scott is still the most illuminating. For it is important to realize what a remarkable achievement it was for Miss Edgeworth to have felt such sympathy for a figure like Sir Condy, since the whole bent and training of her mind was rigidly rationalist and doctrine. The determining influence was that of her father, Richard Lovell Edgeworth, and his significance is clear. We meet him, for instance, in one of his daughter's many admirable letters, her account of a visit to Madame de Genlis:

> Forgive me, my dear Aunt Mary, you begged me to see her with favourable eyes, and I went to see her after seeing her *Rosière de Salency* with the most favourable disposition, but I could not like her; there was something of malignity in her countenance that repelled love, and of hypocrisy which annihilated esteem, and from time to time I saw, or thought I saw, through the gloom of her countenance a gleam of coquetry. But my father judges much more favourably of her than I do; she evidently took pains to please him, and he says she is a person over whose mind he could gain great ascendancy: he thinks her a woman of violent passions, unbridled imagination, and ill-tempered, but *not* malevolent: one who has been so torn to pieces that she now turns upon her enemies, and longs to tear in her turn.

It is hard to be fair to a figure like Edgeworth. A crank, one might argue, is only a genius who doesn't come off. And it is fair to say that Maria never wrote to her father without convincing affection and respect. All the same, it is hard not to read sinister implications into what she reports him as saying of Madame de Genlis—'he is sure she is a person over whose mind he could gain great ascendancy'. One suspects that that was the upshot of all Edgeworth's Rousseauistic experiments in the educating of his children—he gained great ascendancy over their minds. There were twenty-two of them, the products of four separate marriages. Maria was the daughter of the first marriage, the only unhappy one, and adapted herself with surprising ease to three successive stepmothers and succeeding generations of brothers and sisters. There is plenty of evidence that Edgeworth 'gained great ascendancy' over Maria, and it is fair to ask whether his influence was good or bad. It is certainly significant that *Castle Rackrent* was one book in which he had no hand.

It is to him almost certainly that we owe what Madame de Stael lamented as the 'triste utilité' of all his daughter's work. He declared himself that his daughter 'aimed in all her writings to promote the progress of education from the cradle to the grave'. In other words, nearly all she wrote was not just didactic but doctrinaire. On the other hand, if Richard Edgeworth first directed her mind into this channel, there was plenty in the temper of the age to encourage it; and it would need an excessive amount of reading between the lines to establish that Maria was a 'pure' artist confined and spoiled by her father's pressure. Certainly he was a bad influence in specific cases, and it is probably true that what we enjoy in her books nowadays is that element where the moral purpose is least obtrusive. But it would be forcing the issue to argue that there is always in her writing a conflict between the somehow 'pure' artist and the moralist, the two purposes tugging away from one another. Maria Edgeworth was quite happily and deliberately 'one of the blues', a blue-stocking, the last of them perhaps. And if she had had a quite different father, she might well have chosen to write in the very strong blue-stocking tradition of her time—the tradition of Anna Seward, Elizabeth Montagu, Miss Carter, Mrs. Chapone, Mrs. Opie, Mrs. Inchbald, Mrs. Barbauld and Hannah More.

This was, in fact, almost the golden age of the woman-writer in English and Irish and Scottish literature. And of course the first name that springs to mind is that of Jane Austen. Maria Edgeworth has been called an Irish Jane Austen, just as Cooper was called an American Scott. And it may be indeed that Miss Edgeworth comes nearer than any other writer of the time to Miss Austen. But it is still not very near. Miss Austen sent her novels to Edgeworthstown, and Miss Edgeworth admired them, though not without reservations. And of course Jane Austen is a moralist as are all great novelists, in the sense that she thought one kind of human behaviour better than another kind, and wanted in her novels to say so. But of course it is true that she is not a didactic writer, still less doctrinaire. In any case, there was a great gulf between the two women in respect of the lives they led. Nothing could be farther from the truth than to suppose Miss Edgeworth in Edgeworthstown as secluded, as far out of the swim, and confined to as narrow a round, as Miss Austen in Steventon and Chawton. Thanks to her father's fame as an educationist and inventor and later to her own as educationist and novelist, Miss Edgeworth moved continually in the highest European society—the highest both socially and intellectually, since at that time the two still went frequently together. Her poetic enthusiasms were first, Erasmus Darwin, then Scott. (Byron she abominated.) But scientists, engineers, politicians, philosophers, economists—all these she knew, in Ireland, England, France, Switzerland, and conversed with them all on equal terms. It is a striking contrast to the painfully quiet life of Jane Austen.

And this is what makes her letters as a whole better reading than her novels and stories. The finest of all are the letter which describes the visit to Madame de Genlis in 1803[1] and another, of 1831, to the Duchess of Wellington.[2] Some, like the account of a visit to Miss Watts at Leicester,[3] are very much the writing of a novelist—this letter is a novelist's rendering of provincial literary pretentiousness, corrosive yet compassionate. Others permit themselves a more racy and inventive idiom than the novelist could countenance, as in a portrait of Benjamin Constant in 1830:[4]

> I do not like him at all: his countenance, voice, manner, and conversation are all disagreeable to me. He is a fair, *whithky*-looking man, very near-sighted, with spectacles on, and yet looks over the top of his spectacles, *squinching* up his eyes so that you cannot see your way into his mind. Then he speaks through his nose, and with a lisp, strangely contrasting with the vehemence of his emphasis. He does not give me any confidence in the sincerity of his patriotism, nor any high idea of his talents, though he seems to have a mighty high idea of them himself. He has been well called *Le hero des brochures*. We sat beside one another, and I think felt a mutual antipathy.

Or there is the picture of Lavoisier's widow:[5]

> Rejoiced was I that my sisters should have this glimpse of her, and off we drove to her; but I must own that we were disappointed in this visit, for there was a sort of *chuffiness*, and a saw-dust kind of unconnected cut-shortness in her manner, which we did not like. She was almost in the dark with one ballooned lamp, and a semicircle of black men round her sofa, on which she sat cushioned up, giving the word for conversation . . .

Perhaps the best example of the letters at next to the highest level is a letter from Wales in 1802, which moves from an affecting anecdote to an expression of romantic sensibility at

---

[1] *Life and Letters of Maria Edgeworth*, ed. Augustus J. C. Hare, Vol. I, pp. 126–133.

[2] *Ibid.*, Vol. II, pp. 173–176. [4] *Ibid.*, Vol. I, p. 300.

[3] *Ibid.*, Vol. I, pp. 83–85. [5] *Ibid.*, Vol. I, p. 302.

Carnarvon Castle, and then to a fine description of a copper-factory, full of the wonder and awe of the first generation to know the Industrial Revolution.[1] But none of the letters is so germane to the matter of her relations with Scott as one to Auguste de Stael about his Letters on England, in which Miss Edgeworth is the impassioned advocate of Utilitarianism against de Stael's criticisms. (Professor Hausermann, who prints this in *The Genevese Background*, is shocked that she should, writing to the son, permit herself such sarcasm at the expense of the mother; and indeed it is not in the best of taste, though hardly so outrageous as Hausermann suggests.)

It should be plain that this various and lively person, living so near the centre of her age, is not to be summed up as an Irish Jane Austen, nor yet as anti-Romantic or 'Augustan'. She is very exactly a product of the Enlightenment, a category which instructively straddles the divide between the eighteenth century and the nineteenth, between the so-called neo-classical and the so-called Romantic. There might be no need to juggle with these categories if a literary historian like Mr. Cruttwell had not made play with them in order to get his bearings on Scott. We come nearer to understanding Scott's true place among them, by first placing Miss Edgeworth. For Miss Edgeworth and Scott were bound together by mutual esteem, became fast friends and independently acknowledged that each owed much to the other. How did a rationalist and utilitarian like Maria Edgeworth come to terms with the work of one whose genius she admired and extolled? The question is the more interesting because, as we have seen, in *Castle Rackrent* she forestalled Scott not only in what she acknowledged, the painting for the English of the manners and habits of the Irish, as he was to paint the manners of the Scots, but also—and far more important—in building her fiction about a morally weak individual so that in his unsteady destiny should be mirrored the turning-point of two epochs of history.

[1] *Ibid.*, Vol. I, pp. 77–81.

The best test-case is the obvious one, *The Absentee*. And what one notices earliest in this novel are its Austenite elements. There is a point in Chapter IV, for instance, where Miss Edgeworth valuably universalizes the theme announced in her title so as to make of 'absenteeism' more than a merely topical issue and a narrowly Irish concern:

> All this evil had arisen from Lady Beryl's passion for living in London and at watering-places. She had made her husband an *Absentee*—an absentee from his home, his affairs, his duties, and his estate. The sea, the Irish Channel, did not indeed flow between him and his estate; but it was of little importance whether the separation was effected by land or water; the consequences, the negligence, the extravagance, were the same.

This may recall Jane Austen's last unfinished novel *Sanditon*, named after an imaginary watering-place, in which she seems to have intended to censure the sort of person she there calls a 'gad', that is, a gadabout, rootless, wilfully displaced. It was in much the same terms and for the same reasons that Cobbett fulminated against Brighton. And when Scott in *St. Ronan's Well* portrays the same novel milieu of the watering-place he seems to dislike it for much the same reasons, though unfortunately he never quite comes to terms with his distaste so as to define or symbolize it properly.

There are other Austenite elements. Miss Edgeworth's treatment of the commercial nouveau-riche (Mrs. Raffarty at her Tusculum near Bray) recalls Jane Austen's treatment of similar types in, for instance, *The Watsons*; but Miss Edgeworth brings round too easily and complacently the poetic justice of Mr. Raffarty's bankruptcy. Again, Miss Edgeworth's Grace Nugent is, like Fanny Price in *Mansfield Park*, a ward and a dependant; but the Irish novelist doesn't penetrate this predicament as Miss Austen does, nor does she realize what a very advantageous station this was for the author, through her character, to inspect society from. To come nearer the centre of the book, the situation of Lady Clonbrony in relation to her son, Lord Colambre, and her niece, Grace Nugent, is like that of Mrs. Bennet in relation to her daughters Elizabeth and Jane in *Pride and Prejudice.* She makes them blush for her. But in *The Absentee,* just because the mother is seen predominantly through the eyes of a son, not of a daughter, the situation is less painful than in Jane Austen's novel. And Miss Austen is more penetrating and more honest; Elizabeth Bennet is as witty as Grace Nugent, but when she uses her wit to defend her mother her barbs fall harmlessly from the thick skin of Lady de Burgh, whereas Miss Nugent's wit is presented as always effectively putting the unpleasant people out of countenance.

More generally, Maria Edgeworth doesn't, like Miss Austen, maintain a consistent point of view. One aspect of this is her relatively limited use of irony, which in *The Absentee* is only intermittent whereas in *Pride and Prejudice* it is, for good or ill, pervasive. The unsureness in handling irony shows up in a particular feature of Miss Edgeworth's style, at least in the early chapters, her interlarding with literary quotations acknowledged and unacknowledged. When we read in Chapter VII of 'the bit of a broken pipe, which in Ireland never characterises stout labour'[1] or, less excusably, when we hear in Chapter III of Mrs. Dareville's wit, 'Her slings and arrows, numerous as they were and outrageous', the literary reference in the background gives the effect of a poise and detachment which the pointlessness of the allusion reveals as illusory, unearned. In the same way, when in Chapter II Lady Clonbrony objects to Sir Terence O'Fay, the author chooses to echo the Epistle to Arbuthnot: 'No; her ladyship made the most solemn and desperate protestation that she would sooner give up her gala altogether; tie up the knocker; say she was sick; rather be sick or be dead . . .' But to be reminded of Pope adds nothing to our enjoyment and understanding; it signifies noth-

[1] cf. Christopher Smart, 'A Morning Piece': "Strong Labour got up.— With his pipe in his mouth, He stoutly strode over the dale . . .'

ing but a sort of nervous glibness in the writer, a compulsive archness which only masquerades as ironical distance. It is important to remember of course—and in fact this example should bring it home—that irony is not the only, nor the most reliable, way of keeping a consistent point of view. In *Mansfield Park* the hero and heroine are both exempt from irony, as are hero and heroine of *The Absentee*. But Miss Edgeworth's uncertainty shows up in other ways. Probably the clearest example is the relatively minor figure of Sir Terence O'Fay, who at the beginning of the book is presented as the worst type of Irish gentleman in London, but fades out at the end in a haze of indulgent pathos, as a good sort of faithful harum-scarum. This is a good thing in so far as the tone to begin with was insufferably priggish. But it betrays the way in which the book does not hang together quite as it should; some of the issues raised are fobbed off much too easily. It is even difficult to believe, for instance, that after Lord Clonbrony's affairs had got into such a tangle, they could be cleared up merely by returning to Ireland.

On the other hand there are elements in *The Absentee* which sustain a comparison with Jane Austen very well. And I do not have in mind what is called, in a crude sense, Miss Edgeworth's 'social consciousness'. Miss Edgeworth does what Miss Austen is sometimes criticized for ignoring; she deals with the sufferings of the lower orders. But this advantage is more apparent than real. The middle section of the book, dealing with the Irish peasantry deserted by their landlord, is the least lively part, an improving tract only thinly disguised as fiction. Nor do I mean what is something far more substantial, Miss Edgeworth's demi-monde adventuress, Lady Dashfort, who is like Jane Austen's Lady Susan, and rather better. This is a subtle and convincing study, which comes splendidly to life whenever Lady Dashfort opens her mouth. But it is not central to the theme.

More central, or at any rate more interesting, is the figure of

the heiress, Miss Broadhurst. Her good sense and sharp but
never malicious wit remind the reader, once again, of Elizabeth Bennet. But she governs her conduct by principles very
different. She does not look back to Johnson and Cowper,
but forward to Bentham:

> Her father realized his immense fortune by the power and
> habit of constant, bold, and just calculation. The power and habit
> which she had learned from him she applied on a far larger scale.
> With him it had been confined to speculations for the acquisition
> of money; with her it extended to the attainment of happiness. He
> was calculating and mercenary; she was estimable and generous.

There is evasion here. The antithesis contained in the last
sentence is plainly a false one. For if the late Mr. Broadhurst
had been calculating, it is plain from what Miss Edgeworth
says that so is his daughter. She calculates the chances of friendship, for instance, in terms of probable profit and loss to herself,
not financial indeed but emotional. Problems of ethics are amen-
able to the same treatment as problems of commercial speculation. It is the ethos of a commercial, not a landed society. Mickiewicz knew what to say of it, through the mouth of the judge:

> So men approve a title
> And value their connections
> By current estimates,
> As if to strike up a friendship
> Were also a transaction.
> But a sense of personal worth
> Is arrived at only by weighing;
> The beam is only plumb
> With a counterpoise in the pan,
> A worthiness in another.

And if neither Scott nor Jane Austen range themselves so
firmly as this, see so clearly what is involved, yet they do not
evade it as Maria Edgeworth does. Believing that rootedness
matters, that society if healthy is bound together by ties too
subtle and inward to be mirrored on any balance sheet, they

perceive, with Wordsworth, 'arrangements and resources of nature' or 'ways and means of society', which are 'elements as it were of a universe, functions of a living body'. Miss Edgeworth on the other hand sees society as that 'formal machine' which the politician handles, to which Wordsworth opposes his own conviction of infinite subtlety in communal sentiment.

Miss Broadhurst disappears from *The Absentee* after Lord Colambre goes to Ireland; and thereafter all questions of conduct seem to be decided by appeal not to 'calculation' but to the aristocratic principle of honour. This is driven home by the remarks made on Dublin merchants of the type of Raffarty: their error, since they fancy themselves as gentlemen-amateurs of trade not professional tradesmen, is to apply in matters of commerce, the inappropriate standard, honour:

> In the head of a man who intends to be a tradesman to-day and a gentleman tomorrow, ideas of honesty and the duties of a tradesman, and of the honour and accomplishments of a gentleman, are oddly jumbled together, and the characteristics of both are lost in the compound.
>
> He will oblige you, but he will not obey you; he will do you a favour but he will not do you justice; he will do anything to serve you, but the particular thing you order he neglects. He asks your pardon, for he would not, for all the goods in his warehouse, disoblige you; not for the sake of your custom, but he has a particular regard for your family. Economy in the eyes of such a tradesman is, if not a mean vice, at least a shabby virtue, of which he is too polite to suspect his customers, and to which he is proud of proving himself superior. (Chap. VI)

In contrast to these are the 'regular men of business' whom we are asked to esteem—'punctual, frugal, careful, and so forth; with the addition of more intelligence, invention and enterprise than are usually found in Englishmen of the same rank.' The late Mr. Broadhurst differs from these only in being 'bold' where they are 'careful'; and from this point of view to censure him for being 'calculating and mercenary' seems odder than

ever. It amounts to this, apparently: that people should keep
their places; gentlemen should be guided by honour, tradesmen by honesty; but if tradesmen are 'bold' or successful
enough to move up among the gentry, they then become
'mercenary'. This is not what Maria Edgeworth means, but
this is the muddle she provokes in her readers.

In the first chapters, we are invited to make another distinction, between the false honour of Sir Terence O'Fay (who
is, in a sense, a gentleman turned tradesman) and the true
honour of Lord Colambre. But this distinction is never developed, and by the end, with the rehabilitation of Sir Terence,
it is obliterated entirely. It is not hard to see why. At the beginning, the return of the absentees to Ireland is presented as
a patriotic duty, a dictate of honour; and throughout the story
we are asked to admire Colambre for acting in accordance with
honour and humanity, when he returns to Ireland and persuades his family to do the same. We are invited to think that
he comes home in order to rescue his tenants from the oppres-
sion of the middlemen. But the force of this is blunted by the
other argument, insisted on just as much, that it is in the landlord's own interest to return. Enlightened self-interest—that is
the final court of appeal. If the landlord acts in his own best
interest, he will automatically be forwarding the interests of
his tenants. It is the guiding principle of Benthamite optimism.
Hence it is inevitable that questions of honour and patriotic
duty should fade out of the discussion. The whole question of
absenteeism is not a moral question after all, but a piece of
calculation like Mr. Broadhurst's speculations on the Stock
Exchange. Mr. Broadhurst has the last word after all; and if
this is worlds away from the Augustanism of Jane Austen,
it is just as remote from the romanticism of Walter Scott. And
so one sees clearly why Miss Edgeworth, though in *Castle
Rackrent* she had stumbled on that fictional form which was to
be such a pregnant discovery for Scott and his followers, was
unable in her later work to do anything with it.

VII

SCOTT AND THE NOVEL IN IRELAND

ᕯᕯᕯᕯᕯᕯᕯᕯᕯᕯᕯᕯᕯᕯᕯᕯᕯᕯᕯᕯᕯᕯᕯᕯᕯᕯᕯᕯᕯᕯᕯᕯᕯᕯᕯᕯᕯᕯᕯ

IT is curious to think that Miss Edgeworth, at the end of her long life, was in correspondence with Charles Lever, and reading one of his novels aloud to her family. For in a story such as 'Rosanna' from her *Popular Tales*, her standpoint seems at the opposite extreme from his. In this story the secondary villain, Sir Hyacinth O'Brien, is the very spit of Charles O'Malley's uncle; a type for which Miss Edgeworth feels as much contempt as Lever feels affection. In one particular, it is true, Sir Hyacinth differs from a Lever hero: he uses his position to try to seduce a country maiden. And this sufficiently betrays his parent, who is Goldsmith's Squire Thornhill. Indeed there is a great deal of *The Vicar of Wakefield* in the whole structure of this story, and its moral is very similar to that advanced in Goldsmith's Chapter XIX—that is, the happiness and the importance of 'the middle station of life' from which it is a mistake to try to rise. Indeed she had said herself, '*Popular Tales* are not designed for young people— nor for the fashionable *Fine* people in society; but for the respectable and useful middling classes of merchants, manufacturers and farmers, for whose entertainment but few books have been professedly written—The language is necessarily plain and the incidents not such as would interest sentimental novel readers who must have Love, love, love and murder,

murder, murder—'[1] As this suggests, and the comparison with Goldsmith enforces, Miss Edgeworth's attitude is thoroughly of the eighteenth century. 'Without self-approbation, all the luxuries of life are tasteless'—such a judgement reveals the typically Enlightenment compound of strong sense and satisfied complacency.

Yet there are elements in the story which belong to the later century, and it is these which bring about the most obvious difference between 'Rosanna' and *The Vicar of Wakefield*. To be blunt, Dr. Primrose is appealing, where his counterpart, Farmer Gray, is not—is not much more in fact than a tiresome prig. Of course Dr. Primrose is ineffectual where Farmer Gray is not. But it is not just that; part of what we are asked to admire in Farmer Gray is the Victorian virtue of self-help. He is more Tennyson's 'Northern Farmer new style' than 'old style'. In one place Miss Edgeworth reveals that she knows there may be a worse side to the ideal she proposes:

> This generosity quite overpowered Stafford. Generosity is one of the characteristics of the Irish. It not only touched but surprised the Englishman, who, among the same rank of his own countrymen, has been accustomed to strict honesty in their dealings, but seldom to this warmth of friendship and forgetfulness of all selfish considerations.

But it will not quite do. Apparently the author's purpose is to encourage the growth of an Irish yeoman class. But Farmer Gray is not just Goldsmith's Farmer Flamborough transplanted. Potentially, at least, he is a later type, the rural capitalist. As we have seen from *The Absentee*, given the author's standpoint, he could hardly be anything else.

An independent yeomanry or agrarian middle class in Ireland is also the solution for Irish ills which is advanced by William Carleton in *The Emigrants of Ahadarra* (1847), and

---

[1] Letter of 1804, printed in *The Genevese Background* by H. W. Hausermann, p. 68.

in his tendentiousness generally Carleton is very close to Miss Edgeworth. His model, however, is Scott, and he is one of the multitude of writers who aspired to be the Irish Scott. To examine these writers and their books is to get a new sense of Scott's achievement, even at something below his best. It shows how many elements were gathered by Scott into one artistic synthesis, and how impossible it was for anyone but himself to prevent these constituents from separating out again. It prevents us from supposing that Scott supplied a foolproof model or automatic gimmick. Carleton rather touchingly dwelt upon a fancied or real similarity between his own physiognomy and that of his master, and plainly hoped that Scott's mantle had fallen on his shoulders. *The Emigrants of Ahadarra* is not one of Carleton's best novels; much better, for instance, is *Fardorougha the Miser, or the Convicts of Lisnamona* (1837-8), which *The Athenaeum* considered superior to *Père Goriot*. But *The Emigrants of Ahadarra* is more representative. In particular it reveals what was to be one of the besetting faults of the Irish Scotticists, the disintegration of the story into genre-pictures, all too faithfully following Scott's and Miss Edgeworth's avowed purpose of procuring sympathy for the Irish and Scottish nations with their English neighbours. In *The Emigrants of Ahadarra* the story is held up time and again for informative set-pieces of local colour and local custom, such as the spinster's kemp. This is hardly distinguishable from the over-elaboration of stock situations, like the death and funeral of Mrs. M'Mahon, which are dwelt upon through two chapters though they have no bearing on the main theme. This is offered quite simply as a gratuitous emotional wallow, and vicious sentimentality of this sort is the worst thing about Carleton. His readiness to gush about the scenes and figures that he presents for approval (notably about the heroine, who is a stiff and insufferable prig, though Carleton doesn't know it) is in the oddest contrast to his way of being strikingly reticent and impassive about scenes and figures of moral squalor. And the best thing in the book is of this last sort, the three-cornered relationship between Hycy Burke and his parents, in which Carleton also handles dialogue very well indeed. It is good in a way very different from Scott, for it never gives the tang of real speech or racy vernacular, but in a stifled and artificial way it conveys admirably the effect of cut and thrust, of conversational fence, that we associate with some of the best of stage dialogue. On the other hand, try as we may to accept the stilted diction as a consistent convention, we cannot accept 'Her full bust, which literally' [literally!] 'glowed with light and warmth'; and elsewhere we read of a character that 'what he did say was dry and ironical, though not by any means without a tinge of quiet but caustic humour'. These absurdities and tautologies are only extreme instances of a style which is never read without embarrassment and irritation; and it can hardly be denied that Scott was in this respect a baneful precedent.

Carleton did not think well of this book himself, but told his family when he finished it 'that it was only fit for the fire'.[1] But D. J. O'Donoghue, Carleton's biographer, who records this, decides that it is 'one of his best novels':

> In none of Carleton's stories is there such fine character-drawing. Nowhere outside 'The Poor Scholar' and a few of the best of the 'Traits and Stories' are there such moving scenes. It is also the most irreproachable of his books, being almost entirely free from the bad taste, coarseness and rancour which occasionally blemish his works.[2]

O'Donoghue says that this was the general reaction when the novel was first published, and he quotes a contemporary who singles out for praise the drawing of the insufferable heroine Kathleen Cavanagh. I am afraid that the impossible and monstrous 'purity' of this character is almost certainly what is

[1] D. J. O'Donoghue, *The Life of William Carleton* (1896), Vol. II, p. 101.
[2] *Ibid.*

applauded by O'Donoghue and the others as 'good taste', as 'elevating', as 'calculated to do good'. This brings out another facet of Scott's achievement, one which there is nowadays every likelihood will be overlooked; his refusal to point or labour a moral, his trust that whatever was lively to his imagination would have a wholesome moral bearing, just for that reason. This feature of Scott's approach was the one which most stuck in the throat of later generations, which they universally found it impossible to emulate. And not just in Ireland either; when Cooper reviewed Lockhart's *Life*, it was just here—in Scott's indifference to the moral lesson—that he found it necessary to shake his head. This American case (and it could be paralleled in Russia, where Belinsky at just the same time was making the same criticism of Pushkin's prose) should prevent our relating this shift of opinion about moral purpose too narrowly to the change from Regency to more strait-laced Victorian habits of thought and manners, though plainly that has something to do with it as regards Ireland and England.

The best that Scott's admirers could do to justify Scott on this count, and the most liberal interpretation which they could risk of the novelist's moral responsibilities, emerges from a very interesting letter of Miss Edgeworth's.[1] This was written in 1834, apparently in answer to a reasoned private criticism of her own novel *Helen*, and it amounts to a thinking over of the role of convention in prose fiction. Miss Edgeworth's critic had suggested apparently that the moral function of fiction was 'raising the standard of our moral ambition', that is, not driving any particular moral but raising in the mind 'that sort of enthusiasm which exalts and purifies the soul'. Miss Edgeworth associates this effect with the work of Scott; but she declares this laudable effect to be out of her range, and she excuses herself by saying that 'The great virtues, the great vices excite strong enthusiasm, vehement horror, but after all it is not so necessary to warn the generality of mankind against

[1] *Letters*, ed. Hare, Vol. II, pp. 248–255.

these, either by precept and example, as against the lesser faults.'

This understanding of Scott's morality appears also to have been Lever's. Writing in his later years, recalling his student days, he observes:

> We talked of Ivanhoe or Kenilworth, and I can remember too, when the glorious spirit of these novels had so possessed us, that we were elevated and warmed to an unconscious imitation of the noble thoughts and deeds of which we had been reading.

and again, a little later:

> The glorious heroism of Scott's novels was a fine stream to turn into the turbid waters of our worldliness. It was of incalculable benefit to give men even a passing glance of noble devotion, of high-hearted courage, and unsullied purity.[1]

It is significant that it is just the 'romance' of Scott that Lever remembers, not his realism in the description of Scottish manners (which was the side of him that inspired Carleton and the Banim brothers), nor yet Scott's use of the spine-chilling supernatural and sensational (which was to inspire Le Fanu). And this is surely the clue to how Lever expected his early novels to be read—precisely as 'romances', in which we are presented with a simplified, even distorted picture of life, just so that we may be inspired to certain simple but important virtues, courage above all. Charles O'Malley, with all his grievous faults, is offered to the reader as a model to be followed. And at the time Lever's readers were ready to take the story in the way he meant. Lionel Stevenson[2] quotes from a letter sent to Lever by 'the widow of a field officer'. This lady tells Lever how her only son, who was intended for the military profession, had shown 'traits of nervousness and timidity'. But he read *Charles O'Malley* and this (in his mother's words) 'seemed to act like a charm on his whole character,

---

[1] Downey, *Charles Lever. His Life in his Letters* (1906).
[2] Lionel Stevenson, *Dr. Quicksilver*.

inspiring him with a passion for movement and adventure, and spiriting him on to an eager desire for a military life'; so that his performance as a cadet 'has marked him out for an almost hare-brained courage and for a dash and heroism that give high promise for his future'. Lionel Stevenson reports that this letter gave Lever 'intense pleasure'. And no wonder; it is plainly what he was aiming at and hoping for. We may object that 'heroism' and 'dash' are not the same thing, that many of the heroes of common life are not dashing at all, and that courage is all the better if it is not 'harebrained'. Lever's conceptions of courage and honour and heroism are limited ones; but at least it can be admitted that they are true within their limitations, that courage is always a good thing, and that in his early stories of the Irish devil-may-cares Lever was trying (and with success, it appears) to infect his readers with this virtue. It is impossible not to connect this with the 'noble devotion' and 'high-hearted courage' that he had singled out for praise in the romance of Scott.

And indeed Wordsworth had written, in his tract on the Convention of Cintra:

Riddance, mere riddance—safety, mere safety—are objects far too defined, too inert and passive in their own nature, to have ability either to rouse or to sustain. They win not the mind by any attraction of grandeur or sublime delight, either in effort or in endurance; for the mind gains consciousness of its strength to undergo only by exercise among materials which admit the impression of its power,—which grow under it, which bend under it,—which resist,—which change under its influence,—which alter either through its might or in its presence, by it or before it. These, during times of tranquillity, are the objects with which, in the studious walks of sequestered life, Genius most loves to hold intercourse; by which it is reared and supported;—these are the qualities in action and in object, in image, in thought and in feeling, from communion with which proceeds originally all that is creative in art and science, and all that is magnani-

84

mous in virtue.—Despair thinks of *safety*, and hath no purpose; fear thinks of safety; despondency looks the same way:—but these passions are far too selfish, and therefore too blind, to reach the thing at which they aim; even when there is in them sufficient dignity to have an aim.—All courage is a projection from our-selves; however short-lived, it is a motion of hope. But these thoughts bind too closely to something inward,—to the present and to the past,—that is, to the self which is or has been. Whereas the vigour of the human soul is from without and from futurity.

Unfortunately, where Lever is concerned, this cuts both ways; his thoughts were bound very closely to the past. And it is worth dwelling on this, because 'nostalgic' is a word thrown so easily at Scott. It is Lever, however, who shows what the nostalgic is, as opposed to the elegiac.

Of Cromwellian planter stock from County Kilkenny on his mother's side, Lever was born in 1806, the son of a Lancashireman who set himself up as a Dublin master-builder and made a good thing out of it at a time when the city was rapidly expanding. But the Lever we meet in Edmund Downey's memoir as a Trinity College undergraduate from 1822 to 1827, reckless and impulsive, a leader in the social life of the college, an impudent and inventive practical joker—this is already a figure indistinguishable from that of Charles O'Malley as he appears, similarly a Trinity College student, in Lever's novel of that name. A few years later Lever as a medical student, still the wit and the practical joker, walking the wards of the Dublin hospitals, has organized and is running a social club with elaborate ceremonies and mock-rituals of initiation—of the sort that we encounter in another of the early novels, *Jack Hinton*. In the meantime he has visited the German universities and thrown himself ardently into the life of the German student societies with their habits of duelling (which fascinated him always, as it fascinated Pushkin), and, still more in keeping, he has spent a year or so on a mysterious Canadian adventure, going out to Quebec on an emigrant ship from New

Ross, being adopted into a Redskin tribe and only just escaping with his life—a chapter which he drew on later for yet other novels, *Arthur O'Leary* and *Con Cregan*. He gets his medical degree and sets up in practice, only to throw it away and go out to work with energetic devotion in County Clare, fighting a cholera epidemic—still, we perceive, in the manner of his own heroes, who throw off their fecklessness and rise to the really exacting occasion. Then he takes a post as dispensary doctor in Portstewart, shocking the rather stuffy Northern watering-place by his practical jokes, his love of cutting a dash, his headlong horsemanship, his enthusiasm for balls and parties, and his habit of always living beyond his means. In this year, 1832, he marries—and of course, being Charles Lever, it has to be a runaway marriage to a girl without money. Through all this, Lever behaves so exactly as one would expect the creator of Charles O'Malley to behave, that in the end, I think, we grow suspicious. It is as if this life and this personality were deliberately created by Lever—just as he was later to create the lives and the personalities of the heroes of his novels.

Lever had a sort of ideal conception of the man he wanted to be, and did his best to live up to this conception, to embody it in his life as he was later to embody it in his books. One gets the strong impression, after a while, of a man straining to do what is expected of him and keep up the pose—of madcap Dr. Lever, always good for a song and a daring prank, irresponsible and yet in extremities always to be relied on. And indeed the continual flow of vivacity and good spirits was not entirely natural; Lever, it seems, often prepared himself for a social evening with a few grains of opium. And it becomes impossible to overlook an element of wishful thinking, as much in his life at this time as in his first novels a few years later. He is living in a dream world, a world out of the past. As Edmund Downey remarks very much to the point, 'He had spent his early days in an atmosphere charged with recollections of a brilliant era and a mettlesome laughter-loving people'. Precisely. Lever, the nineteenth-century Dublin tradesman's son, was always living in imagination, and trying to impose upon reality, the life of a young eighteenth-century Galway squire. The world he tried to live in was the vanished world of Ireland before the Union, the world of Curran, a world he knew only at second hand, coloured by the wistful anecdotes of older men. The social club, for instance, which he founded in Dublin about 1830, was modelled partly indeed upon the German student societies, but far more closely upon the aristocratic Dublin society of fifty years before, the Monks of the Screw. A young English author who was to achieve fame at almost the same time as Lever, and in a strikingly similar way, who was to be Lever's lifelong rival, was Charles Dickens, who in his early works yearned back similarly towards the recent past, imposing on the Victorian world of the railway train a similarly idealized world, the supposedly more robust and heartily simple England of the stagecoach.

Scott, we are told, squandered his literary earnings and mortgaged them for years to come, in order to set himself up as an old-style baronial landlord in Abbotsford. And so Lever, when he returned from Brussels to Dublin with his name made, installed himself in Templeogue House, kept up a large establishment and entertained lavishly. The difference is that, however much this sort of dream compensation may have coloured Scott's life, he seldom or never let it in to distort his books; the evidence is in the closeness and lavishness with which he documents the past he re-creates. His avid antiquarianism is only a special case of this; and it is all in the strongest contrast to the romances of Lever, which are full of action and of colourful personalities, but otherwise oddly unfurnished.

When Lever was rudely awakened from his dream, it was when as editor of the *Dublin University Magazine* he came under fierce attack from O'Connell and the Repealers, from Carleton and others of the Young Ireland group on the *Nation*, and also from the Tory and Orangeman wing of Irish opinion. The shock of this, which drove him out of Ireland for good, also drove him out of the world of Walter Scott. It was good-bye for good to the Charles Lever who was or aspired to be Charles O'Malley; and for the remaining thirty years of his life Lever was a discouraged and even up to a point an embittered man. In company he was as vivacious as ever, but in his letters and even more in his novels his tone is mostly tart and sombre. *The Daltons*, for instance, an admirably acrid image of *déraciné* life in the spas of Europe, belongs to the world of Thackeray; and it is only the lack of enterprise of the modern reader, not any prejudice against the Scott tradition, which makes this a forgotten book.

Another Irish writer who explicitly invoked the precedent of Scott was Joseph Sheridan Le Fanu. Indeed the two historical novels with which he began his career come nearer than any other Irish novels to challenging Scott on his own ground; or so it must appear at first sight. *The Cock and Anchor: a Chronicle of Old Dublin City*[1] provides, in passing, portraits of Addison, of Swift, and of a famous viceroy, the Earl of Wharton. And similarly *The Fortunes of Colonel Torlogh O'Brien: A Tale of the Wars of King James* (1847) introduces James II, Tyrconnel, Sarsfield, and other historical personages from the period of the Battle of the Boyne. Nevertheless these are not truly historical novels but thrillers in fancy dress.

Torlogh O'Brien himself, for instance, is a character who corresponds very closely in situation to Fergus MacIvor in *Waverley*. Like MacIvor, he is a hereditary chieftain who has been brought up in banishment at the foreign courts, and he returns as MacIvor does, in the train of a dispossessed monarch coming back to claim his own. Scott analyses and penetrates this situation from the inside, showing in MacIvor the clash of two cultures, the one barbaric, the other extremely sophis-

[1] 1845; it was later re-issued with several alterations under the title, *Morley Court*.

ticated. Le Fanu does nothing like this and his Torlogh O'Brien is simply a rather wooden chivalrous hero. Nothing is more betraying than the way Le Fanu ignores the conflict between Roman Catholic and Protestant, a conflict which tore Ireland apart in the periods he writes about as in the period he is writing for. In both these novels a Catholic hero falls in love with a Protestant girl but it apparently never crosses the minds of the heroes nor of their creator that the difference in religious allegiance is a complication in the path of their loves.

The unreality of these stories, their conventionality within the taut and rigid convention of the thriller, is carried right through into the minutiae of style. This is especially true of *Torlogh O'Brien*: 'In a glass darkly' was the title given to a collection of Le Fanu's short stories, and the same metaphor for the imaginative vision appears elaborately in the first chapter of this historical novel. Quite rightly too; for each chapter of the book, at least for the first third of the volume, is as it were a single camera-shot, an ominous landscape, peopled with characters indeed, but all alike, characters and natural features, subdued to the unity of atmosphere. This atmosphere is always the same—foreboding and ominous. And the language that embodies it is similar—a very narrow and highly conventional vocabulary, superbly effective for its one purpose. People are always 'moody', scenes always 'wildly picturesque', ivy crawls on every coign. This is at bottom the vocabulary of the Tale of Terror, but it is governed by a quite serious and coherent aesthetic theory. 'Picturesque' is one of Le Fanu's words; he uses it quite precisely, and his vocabulary of natural description, for instance, adheres to the rules laid down by aesthetic theorists.

As thrillers, both these books have very great merit. The intrigues are ingenious and for the most part internally consistent, the action is rapid, suspense is well managed, and of course Le Fanu can always rise superbly to scenes of the macabre. In *Torlogh O'Brien* there is a spine-chilling account of a death by torture of the strappado and towards the end of *The Cock and Anchor* suspense is sustained relentlessly through chapter upon chapter. Moreover Le Fanu has a splendid grasp of horrific squalor; some of his slum-scenes are as ominous and vivid as those of Dickens—but once again the slums are not specifically *Dublin* slums.

The truth is, Le Fanu is only accidentally Irish. He inhabits from the first the private country of the neurotic. In 1864 he prefaced *Uncle Silas* with a defence of the thriller, speaking of 'the legitimate school of tragic English romance, which has been ennobled, and in great measure founded, by the genius of Sir Walter Scott'. And in a couple of years thereafter Le Fanu had become completely a recluse; he wrote in bed at night and never visited the city from his house in Merrion Square, except occasionally after nightfall to consult the booksellers. Dublin accordingly knew him as 'the Invisible Prince'. It is astonishing to realize that the world of Scott was wide enough for even obsession to find a home there.

Le Fanu is a very expert writer indeed, the most accomplished Irish writer since Maria Edgeworth; there are no longer in him the gaucheries that one finds in Carleton or the Banim brothers or Gerald Griffin. On the other hand there are none of the felicities, vivid through their very awkwardness, that in these writers can compensate by bringing Irish reality quite suddenly and sharply before the reader's eye:

> Never did matter mould itself to mind more agreeably than in the face and form of Andy. Tall, square, slight, loose and bony, he seemed to have been put together carelesssly, or by chance; looking like a bold yet imperfect sketch of a big fellow; and his swarthy visage, entirely devoid of flesh, with the skin fitting tight to his high cheek-bones, and with its mixed expression of good humour, foolishness, fidget, and subtlety, was in keeping with this figure. Even his clothes hung around him at odds and ends, as if they had been tossed on with a pitchfork; and his hat, that part of every man's costume, in its shape and adjustment most

redolent of character, was sometimes pushed back to the very last holding-point of his skull, sometimes dragged down into his eyes, and sometimes only half covering his head, just as the head happened to be humorously, gravely, or rakishly inclined; . . .

In this passage from *Crohoore of the Bill-hook*, the Banims' novel about the County Kilkenny in the period of the White-boy outrages, it is clear that the same *naïveté* which produced the curious expression, 'the very last holding-point of his skull', produced also the excellent 'mixed expression of good-humour, foolishness, fidget, and subtlety'—where the unexpected word 'fidget' is the making of the whole phrase. A similar achievement of this style, which gives the impression of having been knocked together in some provincial yard, is the description of Peery Clancy:

Having failed in every speculation of early life, and become old without credit to himself; having been twice in jail, once for debt, and once for sheep-stealing, Peery Clancy, at fifty years of age, blazed forth a tithe-proctor. He was a waddling, lively old fellow, with a curious struggle of expression in his hard features, and a queer jumble in his manners. The stern bully was on his pursed brow, and in his clenched teeth; but when you looked fixedly at him, there appeared, in his rambling eye, a shuffling consciousness that he had not earned your good opinion, as well as in the general wincing and uneasiness of his person, particularly in the awkward rising and falling, and see-sawing of his arm, as he spoke to you, something like the fidgets of a shame-faced child, that often dreaded and deserved a whipping. A certain air of purse-pride ran, meantime, through all this: and, once in his presence, you would disagreeably feel that he was a man who, however aware he might be of the contempt of the world, possessed, in spite of obloquy, or even of the threat and danger to which he stood exposed, resolution of character to act his part without flinching.

For the sake of the freshness of this vocabulary, its way of hewing close to what it says, one readily tolerates a hero who sets out in all solemnity to save his sweetheart from 'a fate worse than direct death'; a peasant who squats, 'the aft part of his large and gaunt person, resting on his heels'; and a turf cabin which 'differed but little from the open moor without, from which it had only recently been deducted; . . .'

In fact there are all sorts of special considerations to be borne in mind when considering the use of English by an Irish writer, at least if we use 'Irish' as Carleton did when he wrote in a letter, 'The only three names which Ireland can point to with pride are Griffin's, Banim's, and—do not accuse me of vanity when I say—my own!' Anglo-Irish writers like Maria Edgeworth, Le Fanu, Lever can be judged by the same standards as their English contemporaries, but with writers only one generation or less away from Gaelic culture the position is quite different. Instructive in this connection is Carleton's portrait, in *The Emigrants of Ahadarra*, of Finigan, the 'philomath' and drunken hedge-schoolmaster. He uses habitually a florid eloquence which is ludicrous. And Carleton makes fun of it, yet he also makes Finigan the shrewdest character in his story, and sometimes Finigan's English is no longer ludicrous but truly eloquent. If James Sutherland is right[1] when he argues that in the late eighteenth century English prose became Gibbonian or Johnsonian, moving away from conversation, above all because of pressure from the Scottish writers whose speech was in Scots (the historian Robertson is his case in point). then the flaccidity of Scott's prose can be explained on the same terms as the prose of Robertson; in neither case could speech usage be a check or guide to the written language, because the language the writers spoke and heard spoken was much of the time not English at all. And the same argument applies with all the more force to writers who had spoken and heard spoken Irish Gaelic rather than English. And so it should come as no surprise when, in *The Collegians* of Gerald Griffin, as in so many

[1] James Sutherland, 'Some Aspects of Eighteenth-Century Prose', in *Essays on the Eighteenth Century presented to David Nichol Smith*, p. 108.

of Scott's novels, there is a yawning gulf between the vitality of the peasants' brogue and the frigidity of the more genteel dialogue, not to speak of the author's own idiom in narration and description. Griffin's style is always excessive:

Before her lay the gigantic portals of the Shannon, through which the mighty river glided forth with a majestic calmness, to mingle with the wide and waveless ocean that spread beyond and around them. On her right arose the clifted shores of Clare, over which the broad ball of day, although sometimes hidden from her sight, seemed yet, by refraction, to hold his golden circlet suspended amid a broken and brilliant mass of vapours. Eily kept her eyes fixed in admiration on the dilated orb, until a turn in the cave concealed the opening from her view, and she could only see the stream of light behind, as it struck on the jagged and broken walls of the orifice, and danced upon the surface of the agitated waters.

This has undoubtedly an ornate beauty of its own, yet 'the broad ball of day' and 'the dilated orb' are doubtless things too highly seasoned for even the lustiest modern palate. At other times the writing recalls nothing so much as *The Young Visiters*:

Light and laughter—mirth and music—plenteous fare and pleasant hearts to share it, were mingled in the dining-room on this occasion. Mrs. Chute presided; the 'old familiar faces', of Mr. Cregan, Mr. Creagh, Mr. Connolly, Doctor Leake, and many others, were scattered among the guests, and every eye seemed lighted up, to contribute its portion of gaiety to the domestic jubilee. A cloud of vapour, thin and transparent as a Peri's sighs, arose from the dishes which adorned the table, and was dissipated in the air above. The heavy moreen window-curtains were let down, the servants flew from place to place like magic, the candles shed a warm and comfortable lustre upon the board, and the clatter of plates, the jingling of glasses and decanters, the discomfiture of provision, and the subdued vigour with which all this was accomplished, considering the respectability of the guests, was really astonishing.

This is babu's English. One sets against it such vivid and un-embarrassed prose as the description of Lowry Looby in Chapter IV. But it is not a matter of balancing the good against the bad. For Griffin's (and less certainly the Banims') is a case that calls for special pleading, just as the babu's does. What we have in both cases is an un-English mind trying to express it-self in a language wholly foreign to its most intimate habits of thought and feeling. As late as 1937 and 1942, Joseph Ranson found just this sort of inspired gibberish still being sung on the coast of Wexford:

> Your aid I crave, you Muses; I pray, lend no excuses;
> But in spite of my confusion, my slender quill do guide;
> And order a proclamation, to state the desolation,
> And the woeful lamentation that we heard of Malahide . . .

> The eighteenth of December, it was the fateful date,
> The sky had a gloomy aspect, pregnated with sad fate;
> O'er the celestial orbs of light great sable clouds were drew,
> As in the east horizon a ship appeared in view . . .

What in the mouth of an Englishman would be the most ex-hausted of clichés strikes these Irishmen as a novel and excit-ing figure of speech, and is used by them exuberantly to convey a genuine experience. Reach-me-down locutions like 'slender quill', 'celestial orbs of light' are not, as they would be in English poetry, symptoms of slack feeling and listless thought, but as it were re-minted and awkwardly alive. And this is as true of some of Griffin's prose as of this folk-poetry. The pretentious rant of his villain, Hardress Cregan, is bad on any account, if only because we could imagine it written by an Englishman. But passages like that on the 'portals of the Shannon', or the 'domestic jubilee', with its 'cloud of vapour, thin and transparent as a Peri's sighs'—these could not have been written by an Englishman, and exhibit a native eloquence making sense and poetry out of a sort of artifice long grown faded and cumbrous in the place of its origin. Of course it would be absurd to pretend that the case for Scott's style can be pushed at all so far on the same lines; yet it is only fair to realize that for him also English could not be other than an exclusively literary language, with all that that entails in terms of awkwardness and enervation.

The Collegians is the basis of Boucicault's play *Colleen Bawn* and Benedict's opera *Lily of Killarney*. C. H. Herford describes it by saying, a 'somewhat melodramatic story of the Amy Robsart type serves as framework for a profusion of admirable studies in Irish peasant character.'[1] *Kenilworth* had appeared in 1821, five years before Griffin started *The Collegians*; but a modern reader may think first not of Amy Robsart but of Dreiser's *American Tragedy*. And this is fairer to Griffin; for his story of the low-born secret wife betrayed and murdered by her high-born husband is used by Griffin, as not by Scott, to establish a whole social hierarchy in all its niceties of class-distinction. It is this that gives to Griffin's story of Munster society a depth and density such as Scott was not concerned with; this reminds us of *Middlemarch* rather, and makes it a novel of manners in Lionel Trilling's sense:

> One of the things which makes for substantiality of character in the novel is precisely the notation of manners, that is to say, of class traits modified by personality.[2]

This is the point of the following passage, for instance:

> Such, in happier days than ours, was the life of a Munster farmer. Indeed, the word is ill adapted to convey to an English reader an idea of the class of persons whom it is intended to designate, for they were and are, in mind and education, far superior to persons who occupy that rank in most other countries. Opprobrious as the term 'middleman' has been rendered in our time, it is certain that the original formation of the sept was both

[1] C. H. Herford, *The Age of Wordsworth*, p. 126.
[2] Lionel Trilling, *The Liberal Imagination*.

natural and beneficial. When the country was deserted by its gentry, a general promotion of one grade took place among those who remained at home. The farmers became gentlemen and the labourers became farmers, the former assuming together with the station and influence, the quick and honourable spirit, the love of pleasure, and the feudal authority which distinguished their aristocratic archetypes, while the humbler classes looked up to them for advice and assistance, with the same feeling of respect and of dependence which they had once entertained for the actual proprietors of the soil. The covetousness of landlords themselves, in selling leases to the highest bidder, without any enquiry into his character or fortune, first tended to throw imputations on this respectable and useful body of men, which in progress of time swelled into a popular outcry, and ended in an act of the legislature for their gradual extirpation. There are few now in that class as prosperous, nor many as intelligent and high-principled, as Mr. Daly.

The passage is unfortunately ambiguous, for to the English reader who does not know, from *The Absentee* or elsewhere, the Irish meaning of 'middleman', it remains unclear whether the Dalys are farmers-become-gentlemen, or labourers-become-farmers. In fact they are the former, as are other families in the novel, the Cregans and the Chutes; and Mr. Daly's assumption of the responsibilities of the gentry is to be contrasted with Mr. Cregan's assumption only of their privileges:

'But I was speaking', Mr. Daly resumed, 'of the family pride of the Cregans. It was once manifested by Hardress's father in a manner that might make an Englishman smile. When their little Killarney property was left to the Cregans, amongst many other additional pieces of display that were made on the occasion, it behoved Mr. Barney Cregan to erect a family vault and monument in his parish churchyard. He had scarcely, however, given directions for its construction, when he fell ill of a fever, and was very near enjoying the honour of hanselling the new cemetery himself. But he got over the fit, and made it one of his first cares to saunter out as far as the church and inspect the mansion which had been prepared for his reception. It was a handsome Gothic monument, occupying a retired corner of the churchyard, and shadowed over by a fine old sycamore. But Barney, who had no taste for the picturesque, was deeply mortified at finding his piece of sepulchral finery thrown so much into the shade. "What did I or my people do," he said to the architect, "that we should be sent skulking into that corner. I paid my money, and I'll take my own value for it." The monument was accordingly got rid of, and a sporting flashy one erected opposite the gateway, with the Cregan crest and shield (in what herald's office it was picked up I cannot take upon me to say) emblazoned on the frontispiece. Here it is to be hoped, the aspiring Barnaby and his posterity may one day rest in peace'.

There is plenty of this sort of thing, especially in the first hundred pages or so, where the characters are bedded firmly into the social structure even as they are set in motion; so that Herford is wrong to treat the story merely 'as framework'. His error is as common among admirers of Scott and the Scott tradition as among their detractors, the assumption that 'plot' cannot at best be other than a convenience; the betrayal and murder of Eily constitutes the one right and adequate vehicle for what the novel is about, its plot is at one with its theme.

'Such, in happier days than ours . . .'—this belongs to another aspect of the book, again one that is most evident in the earlier pages. *The Collegians* is presented as a historical novel, set back fifty years or so before the time at which it is written; and the very first chapter, a threnody on the decline of Garryowen, is bathed in a cloying nostalgia. Indeed we get a sort of nostalgia inside nostalgia. For the story is set in the vanished never-never land of Garryowen's heyday, yet one of the characters is allowed to yearn back even farther:

'Heaven be with ould times! There is nothin' at all there as it used to be, Master Kyrle. There isn't the same weather there, nor the same peace, nor comfort, nor as much money, nor as strong whiskey, nor as good *piatees*, nor the gentlemen isn't so pleasant in themselves, nor the poor people so quiet, nor the boys so divartin', nor the girls so coaxin', nor nothin' at all is there as it used to be formerly. Hardly I think, the sun shines as bright in the day; an' nothin' shows itself now by night, neither spirits nor good people. In them days, a man couldn't go a lonesome road at night without meetin' things that would make the hair of his head stiffen equal to bristles. Now you might ride from this to Dingle without seeing anything uglier than yourself on the way.'

This nostalgia is really irrelevant to the book, and indeed it disappears as soon as the story gets under way. I suspect that Griffin was trapped into it by emulation of Scott, for he shared the admiration that was felt for Scott by all his Irish contemporaries.

But Griffin's true interests are very different from Scott's. And because of this his 'profusion of admirable studies in Irish peasant character'—Lowry Looby, Myles na Coppaleen, Fighting Poll o' the Reeks, and Foxy Dunat (in for instance his brilliant and affecting discourse on 'piatez' in Chapter XXX)—exist in something better than a 'framework'; they take their places in a solid and flexible unified structure which is none the worse for not being one of Scott's structures.

By contrast, in *Crohoore of the Bill-hook*, towards the end even the pretence of the ludicrous plot is virtually abandoned, and whole chapters are given up to genre-pictures connected very tenuously indeed with what purports to be the main action—a company of professional beggars; Fair-day in Kilkenny; a rustic wooing. [And this last, incidentally (Chapter XII), is intolerably condescending and ugly in tone—the Banims, writers from the people, ridicule their countrymen for foreign consumption far more than do the writers of the Ascendancy.] Similarly, the very title of Carleton's shorter pieces, *Traits and Stories of the Irish Peasantry*, reveals the double motive behind their writing, the two stools they are to fall between; are these indeed 'stories' or pieces of reportage? To be sure, the interest of Carleton's material is so great, and his own temperament and situations are so arrestingly peculiar, that it would be a sort of pedantry to ask whether the value of these astonishing productions is anthropological or literary. Carleton, we may say, fails to be an Irish Scott because he is himself a character out of Scott, he is part of Scott's subject-matter. The telling evidence here is his absorbing *Autobiography*. Mrs. Cashel Hoey compared Carleton in his autobiography with Rousseau in terms of 'the startling candour' and 'the absence of *mauvause honte*' with which both writers reveal themselves. This is just. And Carleton's memoir is not damned by a comparison with Rousseau's pupil Tolstoy, in his autobiographical writings. (There is however an example nearer home—the vanity and simplicity, going along with profundity and shrewdness, is also what we find in Goldsmith.) And yet there is a great difference between Carleton's autobiography on the one hand, Rousseau's and Tolstoy's on the other—Carleton gives the picture not just of a soul but of a society. And Mrs. Hoey is short-sighted to lay such stress on Carleton's ingenuousness in thinking that the world owed him a living. The autobiography shows that this was not just a quirk of vanity on Carleton's part; it was taken for granted by the society into which he was born, which accepted the special privileges attending the function of bard and story-teller. And the prickly self-pity and resentment which shows through all Carleton's later career in Dublin shows how impossible it was for him to come to terms with a mercantile society in which the purveyor of literature had to sell his wares on the open market like any other producer. This is an aspect of the change-over from a barbaric to a commercial society which Scott did not dwell upon.

Scott's precedent, which the Irish novelists understandably believed to be peculiarly apposite to their problems and purposes, in fact did not serve them well. And at the end of the century, though Standish O'Grady was still pursuing the mirage of 'an Irish Scott', the influence that proved fruitful through George Moore's *The Untilled Field* was that of Turgenev. As has been realized, this model, embraced also by Daniel Corkery, by O'Faolain and O'Connor, was appropriate partly because it came out of a society which was like Irish society in that the middle classes were not substantial enough to fill in the social canvas between landowner and peasant. Only *The Real Charlotte* of Somerville and Ross can stand with *The Collegians* as a delineation of a rural middle class milieu in Ireland; and as 'a novel of manners' this too is constructed on a model which owes as little to Turgenev as to Scott. It is interesting to reflect that since Turgenev as well as Scott acknowledged a debt to Miss Edgeworth, Irish fiction can be said to have come out from under the cloak of the mistress of Edgeworthstown at least as fairly as all Russian fiction can be said, in a famous phrase, to come out from the cloak of Gogol.

VIII

THE LEATHERSTOCKING NOVELS

ᘒᘒᘒᘒᘒᘒᘒᘒᘒᘒᘒᘒᘒᘒᘒᘒᘒᘒᘒᘒᘒᘒᘒᘒᘒᘒᘒᘒᘒ

COOPER in his own day was called 'the American Scott.' Lockhart decided he was the best of all Scott's imitators and Balzac coupled the two names together in a momentous appreciation of *The Pathfinder*. Cooper himself was proud enough of the title until he was incensed by Lockhart's *Life of Scott*. (Lockhart printed a journal-entry by Scott, dating from a period in the eighteen-twenties when the pair of them, 'the Scottish lion and the American lion', were being feted together in Paris. Scott remarked that Cooper had the typically American 'manner or absence of manner'. In Lockhart this became 'manners, or absence of manners'.) But times have changed; and in our own day when Marius Bewley wants to make a case for Cooper, he does so by angrily putting the blame for neglect of Cooper precisely on this label, 'the American Scott', and arguing, on the very slender grounds of Cooper's bad first novel *Precaution*, that Cooper's idea of plot came to him from Jane Austen, not from Scott at all.[1] When Mr. Bewley reprinted his essay in *The Eccentric Design*, he rightly omitted this and other disparaging references to Scott, but his first version is invaluable for showing what delicate ground it is, this whole question of Cooper's relation to the Scott tradition. On the one hand Leslie Fiedler can write:

[1] Scrutiny, Vol. XIX, No. 2.

A chief technical problem for American novelists has been the adaptation of nontragic forms to tragic ends. How could the dark vision of the American—his obsession with violence and all his embarrassment before love—be expressed in the sentimental novel of analysis as developed by Samuel Richardson or the historical romance as practised by Sir Walter Scott? These sub-genres of fiction, invented to satisfy the emotional needs of a merchant class in search of dignity or a Tory squirearchy consumed by nostalgia, could only by the most desperate expedients be tailored to fit American necessities.[1]

On the other hand, we read:

Cooper, for all his historical importance, his status as the founding father of American fiction, cannot compare in literary merit with the founding father he derived from—Scott—or from other founding fathers like Lermontov or Manzoni; his importance, which is enormous, is historical; fascinating to read about, he remains a bore to read. His significance is that he established the themes that seem to have preoccupied American novelists constantly since his day.[2]

Mr. Fiedler is ready to allow that Cooper never 'proved capable of achieving high art'; and Henry Bamford Parkes is not worried by having to concede that Cooper's myth continues to this day more influential on more people than any other (for in the Lone Ranger and Tonto on the T.V. screen we see Leatherstocking and Chingachgook still), at the same time as he reproaches Marius Bewley and Yvor Winters for pretending that Cooper is a great writer. It is best to say at the start that, however much I may differ from Mr. Winters and Mr. Bewley at specific points, I am impenitently of their opinion that Cooper is a very great writer indeed. Certainly, to investigate his relations with Scott is not the only way into seeing his greatness;

[1] Leslie Fiedler, 'The Novel and America'. *Partisan Review*, Winter 1960; reprinted as Introduction to *Love and Death in the American Novel*.
[2] *Times Literary Supplement*, Friday, Nov. 6th, 1959.

yet between Cooper's admirers to whom Scott is an embarrassment, and Scott's admirers for whom Cooper is damned by the comparison, there is a confusion which seems to mirror the larger confusion about how much either writer is worth in himself. And there is so much reason to think that approaching Cooper with Scott in mind may be worthwhile.

THE PIONEERS

Cooper was also acquainted with Mickiewicz, and in 1830 in Rome Mickiewicz frequented Cooper's household so markedly that it was rumoured he was to marry the American's daughter. There are grounds for thinking that more may yet be discovered about this connection. Cooper was very active on his friend's behalf at the time of the November rising in Poland, and addressed to the Americans an appeal for aid to the Poles. It has been suggested that the Polish poet took hints from Cooper's *Spy* for his *Konrad Wallenrod*.

Certainly, to a reader who knows both works, Chapter XXII of Cooper's *Pioneers*, the earliest of the Leatherstocking books, is likely to recall the passages which lead up to the bear-hunt in *Pan Tadeusz*. There is no question of 'influence', narrowly considered; simply, both works are full of the sense of wilderness, of the lavishness of natural provision for man, and of the exactly intricate natural order which is disturbed by man's intrusion. The very type of the sportsman which is central to both the Polish poem and the American novel, drawing on the familiar but poignant paradox by which man is never so intimate with wild nature as when he hunts it down, binds the two works together and reveals how much the two men had in common. It is partly because both the Lithuanian wilderness and the American are forested that we do not relate this feature in both Cooper and Mickiewicz, as perhaps the contemporary reader did, to Scott's descriptions of the Highland wilderness, for instance in *Rob Roy*. But if this in Scott was to either or both of the others a precedent, each of them surpassed their master, not just in the closeness and vividness of their evocations, but in binding them up far more closely with the action and with what the action symbolizes, a confrontation of two incompatible norms of sentiment and conduct.

Yet *The Pioneers* is of all the Leatherstocking books the one which in structure most resembles the structures of Scott. For here the two norms are represented, as they are by Scott, as the past and the future confronting each other at a turning point in history. What Cooper was to discover—and this was to determine the whole exfoliation of the Leatherstocking saga—was that in American history this turning-point was to be repeated again and again as the frontier moved west. For at the frontier, wherever and whenever found, the past is symbolized by the settlement behind, the future by the wilderness in front. When in the later Leatherstocking books Cooper chose to operate always beyond the settled frontier, the structure of Scott could serve him no longer.

The Pioneers falls short of *Waverley* in that Cooper does not succeed in contriving a weak central character whose wavering from one allegiance to another shall mirror the confrontation of loyalties. His youthful hero, the disguised younger Effingham, is as shadowy and unsatisfactory as were to be all the later figures which Cooper cast for the Romantic lead; and it is he who shuttles to and fro between Leatherstocking and his Indian colleague on the one hand, and Judge Temple on the other, who stands for the settled law and order which Leatherstocking cannot abide. In fact it is the Judge himself who is poised uncertainly between the two extremes, between the lawlessness of the settlements themselves (represented by his kinsman Richard Jones) and the lawlessness of Leatherstocking's wilderness. But the existence of the unsatisfactory young Effingham serves to displace the Judge and obscure his centrality. However, *The Pioneers* continues to resemble *Waverley*, chiefly because Cooper's sympathies are in this book equally divided, in a way which was common for Scott and in tune with Scott's relaxed and permissive temperament, whereas it is uncharacteristic of the more rigid and irascible Cooper. Already in *The Pioneers*, though Cooper's sympathies are divided, it is plain that his principles must sway him decisively to one allegiance rather than the other, to the wilderness rather than the settlements; and so this first of the Leatherstocking novels contains all the others in embryo.

THE LAST OF THE MOHICANS

D. H. Lawrence was indubitably right to insist that the five Leatherstocking novels should be read in the order in which they were composed: *The Pioneers, The Last of the Mohicans, The Prairie, The Pathfinder, The Deerslayer*. Read in this order, as Lawrence said, they represent a steady diminution of reality and a steady crescendo of beauty—or, as may be said, of myth. The series as a whole constitutes a uniquely clear case of how imagination gradually modifies actuality, steadily replacing the factual truth of record or chronicle by the imaginative truth of poem and myth.

To those who have blundered into reading the series in the reverse order, the process is even clearer if less enthralling. Certainly to come to *The Last of the Mohicans* after the apotheosis of *The Pathfinder* and *The Deerslayer*, or even after the set-piece, as in a saint's life, of Leatherstocking's death at the end of *The Prairie*, is to realize with a shock how far Cooper was, at the beginning of his venture, from understanding where it was to lead him. *The Last of the Mohicans* is sub-titled, as it seems almost defiantly, 'a narrative'—'A Narrative of 1757'. And in his Preface, Cooper insists that his intention is, in the bleakest most uncompromising way, realistic:

> The reader who takes up this volume in expectation of finding an imaginary and romantic picture of things which never had an

existence, will probably lay it aside disappointed. The work is exactly what it professes to be in its title page—a narrative.

Though Cooper found it necessary to warn his first readers thus sternly, it must have come to them with much less of a shock than it does to us, to find Leatherstocking here naked of all the glamour that was to be cast about him so abundantly in the later books. In *The Last of The Mohicans* Leatherstocking is above all a bloodthirsty and superstitious figure, living by a code which the novelist disapproves of. Apart from anything else—and this is most striking in view of what was to come afterwards—Leatherstocking in this novel is a philistine. In Chapter VI, for instance, he reflects upon his private sanctuary behind a waterfall:

'Ay! there are the falls on the two sides of us, and the river above and below. If you had daylight it would be worth the trouble to step up on the height of this rock, and look at the perversity of the water. It falls by no rule at all; sometimes it leaps, sometimes it tumbles; there it skips; here it shoots; in one place 'tis white as snow, and in another 'tis green as grass; hereabouts it pitches into deep hollows, that ramble and quake the 'arth; and thereaway it ripples and sings like a brook, fashioning whirlpools and gullies in the old stone, as if 'twas no harder than trodden clay. The whole design of the river seems disconcerted. First it runs smoothly, as if meaning to go down the descent as things were ordered; then it angles about and faces the shores; nor are there places wanting where it looks backward, as if unwilling to leave the wilderness, to mingle with the salt! Ay, lady, the fine cob-web-looking cloth you wear at your throat, is coarse, and like a fish net, to little spots I can show you, where the river fabricates all sorts of images, as if, having broke loose from order, it would try its hand at every thing. And yet what does it amount to? After the water has been suffered to have its will for a time, like a head-strong man, it is gathered together by the hand that made it, and a few rods below, you may see it all, flowing on steadily towards the sea, as was foreordained from the first foundation of the 'arth!'

The touching distinction of this passage is in the way the speaker acknowledges a sort of beauty and impressiveness in the scene, which his opinions and convictions leave no room for. The beautiful sentence about how 'the river fabricates all sorts of images', in reticulations so fine that against it cambric seems 'like a fish net', represents a perception for which there is no room in a view of nature which depends upon 'the argument from Design', a view of nature which will acknowledge it to be beautiful only when it evinces symmetry and order which argue the wisdom of its Creator. Expressions like 'perversity', 'no rule at all . . .', 'the whole design . . . seems disconcerted', 'loose from order', 'what does it amount to?' show that the speaker is employing an outdated, a pre-Romantic set of standards. And Cooper underlines this:

> While his auditors received a cheering assurance of the security of their place of concealment, from this untutored description . . ., they were much inclined to judge differently from Hawk-eye, of its wild beauties. But they were not in a situation to suffer their thoughts to dwell on the charms of natural objects; . . .

In none of the later novels would Cooper thus permit his genteel characters to condescend to the hunter; nor in those books does he allow that the hunter's responsiveness to natural beauty was in any way limited.

Leatherstocking's philistinism is brought out also by his exchanges with the New England choirmaster, David Gamut. Gamut, as his name implies, is a Jonsonian humour such as Scott's Peregrine Touchwood (in *St. Ronan's Well*). There is one of these in nearly every one of Cooper's novels, and very tedious they are. In *The Pathfinder* it is Mabel Dunham's uncle, the saltwater sailor who interminably rings the changes upon his contempt for the freshwater sailors of the Great Lakes; in *The Prairie* it is (most fatuous of them all) Dr. Battius, the naturalist, who incongruously accompanies the squatter Ishmael Bush. These figures appear to represent Cooper's gestures towards comic relief; but it is impossible to think that anyone ever found them humorous. Gamut is much the most supportable of them—partly because he has little to say and only hovers on the fringes of the story, but more because, as explicitly a representative of the Arts, he is made to reveal very clearly one of Leatherstocking's limitations. For Leatherstocking is made to treat him and his function with contempt and a sort of baffled derision. And while the hunter is at one point (Chapter XII) allowed to score over him, in rejecting his Calvinist idea of providence, more telling is the exchange in Chapter XXVI, where Leatherstocking leaves Gamut in peril:

'If, however, they take your scalp, as I trust and believe they will not, depend on it, Uncas and I will not forget the deed, but revenge it, as becomes true warriors and trusty friends.'

'Hold!' said David, perceiving that with this assurance they were about to leave him; 'I am an unworthy and humble follower of one, who taught not the damnable principle of revenge. Should I fall, therefore, seek no victim to my manes, but rather forgive my destroyers: and if you remember them at all, let it be in prayers for the enlightening of their minds, and for their external welfare!'

The scout hesitated, and appeared to muse deeply.

'There is a principle in that,' he said, 'different from the law of the woods! and yet it is fair and noble to reflect upon.' Then, heaving a heavy sigh, probably among the last he ever drew in pining for the condition he had so long abandoned, he added— 'It is what I would wish to practise myself, as one without a cross of blood, though it is not easy to deal with an Indian, as you would with a fellow christian. God bless you friend; I do believe your scent is not greatly wrong, when the matter is duly considered, and keeping eternity before the eyes, though much depends on the natural gifts and the force of temptation'.

Wooden as this is, it is very significant, especially the phrase about 'pining for the condition he had so long abandoned'. For while it is true that the hunter was never in the later books to sigh for the condition of a civilian in the settlements, he was increasingly to honour and practise the pacific Christian injunction to turn the other cheek. And this passage shows how far Cooper was at this time from conceiving, what he was later to contend for so warmly, that this precept along with the rest of Christian morality was not only possible to, but positively enforced by, life in the wilderness.

As Yvor Winters says, the plot of *The Last of the Mohicans* is in one sense a good one. The events, to use Aristotelean terminology, have a probable or necessary connection one with another; there is suspense, reversal and surprise; and the action unrolls itself at a pace that is almost brisk. But it is the plot merely of an adventure-story; the action is at no point the vehicle of a theme. For in this sense the story has no theme, and this is what one means, indeed, by calling it, without compromise, 'realistic'. The love of the young Redskin Uncas for the white girl Cora has, for instance, none of the thematic significance of the similar relationship in *The Wept of Wish-ton-Wish*, where it is similarly consummated in the only way Cooper's imagination could tolerate, by death. Still less has it the weight and centrality of the relationship between Edward Waverley and Flora MacIvor, where the possibility of a marriage between them is symbolic of what is Scott's massive and urgent theme, the possible marrying of two historical and divergent cultures. In fact, of course, since Cora has to be given a touch of the tar-brush before she can be permitted even a symbolic consummation with her Redskin lover, this thread in the plot leads at once into the murkiest most unsavoury element in Cooper, his attitude to sexual relations and the colour bar. His other heroine, the swooning imbecilic child-bride Alice, is a more ghastly symptom than the worst child-women of Dickens or Thackeray, of a pathologically perverted attitude to sex. If the case were simply that Cooper cannot conceive of sexual relations athwart the colour-bar, there would be no point in making a fuss about it. But the truth is that here,

as in *The Prairie* and even in *The Pathfinder*, Cooper's imagination continually plays with the possibility, and invites it in
order to repress it hysterically.

It is this, and this alone, which constitutes the villainy of the
powerfully drawn Huron villain, Magua (as, though more
weakly, of the Teton villain of *The Prairie*, Mahtoree). Magua,
though cast for the villain, is in fact the only character in *The
Last of the Mohicans* who acts consistently in accord with a
reasonable moral conviction:

'The Spirit that made men, coloured them differently', com-
menced the subtle Huron. 'Some are blacker than the sluggish
bear. These he said should be slaves; and he ordered them to work
for ever, like the beaver. You may hear them groan, when the
south winds blow, louder than the lowing buffaloes, along the
shores of the great salt water, when the big canoes come and go
with them in droves. Some he made with faces paler than the
ermine of the forests: and these he ordered to be traders; dogs
to their women, and wolves to their slaves. He gave this people
the nature of the pigeon; wings that never tire; young, more plen-
tiful than the leaves on the trees, and appetites to devour the earth.
He gave them tongues like the false call of the wild-cat; hearts
like rabbits; the cunning of the hog, (but none of the fox), and
arms longer than the legs of the moose. With his tongue, he stops
the ears of the Indians; his heart teaches him to pay warriors to
fight his battles; his cunning tells him how to get together the
goods of the earth; and his arms enclose the land, from the shores
of the salt water, to the islands of the great lake. His gluttony
makes him sick. God gave him enough, and yet he wants all.
Such are the pale-faces.'

Magua, who goes on to argue that, as God made the black
man a slave and the white man a trader, so he made the red man
a hunter, here employs from the opposite side of the fence the
argument of Hurry Harry, the white hunter in *The Deerslayer*,
for whom the redskin is less than human. And it is true that in
that book Leatherstocking is given a nobler philosophy than

this. But he has no such philosophy in *The Last of the Mohicans*. And in fact, within the world of that book, Magua's argument is unanswerable.

He behaves more nobly by his lights than anyone else in the book. (Hayward, for instance, the young British officer, comes under no censure for tempting Magua with 'firewater', and it is plain that we are meant to think the better of him for revising his feelings about Cora when he learns of her Negro strain.) But of course what finally throws the moral perspectives wholly awry is the elegiac interest which gives the book its title. For Magua might here be speaking for the Mohicans, since it was the white man's rapacity and double-dealing which dispossessed and decimated them. For this reason the full-dress elegiac spectacle at the end of the book, the funeral for the last Mohican, Uncas, rings very hollow indeed.[1] It is instructive, and a salutary check to any disposition to idealize the age for which Cooper wrote, to realize that it was this book, *The Last of the Mohicans*, so much at the mercy of moral anarchy in its author and his subject, which brought fame to Cooper and made his name a household word throughout Europe.

THE PRAIRIE

This novel, except for the first chapter and the last three, labours under the disadvantage of a style which is peculiarly uncouth even for Cooper. The staple of Cooper's style, as of Scott's, is the style of Gibbon very far gone in decay; its orotund gentility especially conspicuous and inappropriate because of the rough manners in the societies that Cooper chose to depict. Still, though it is vicious in itself (because used as

[1] The only moment when the elegiac note rings true is much earlier in the book in Chapter XIII, where 'The grey light, the gloomy little area of dark grass, surrounded by its border of brush, beyond which the pines rose in breathless silence, apparently, into the very clouds, and the death-like stillness of the vast forest, were all in unison to deepen such a sensation.'

means to an end so different from the ends of Gibbon), it is the style of the period, and it can be accepted as a convention which, however wastefully tedious, is at least internally consistent. But in *The Prairie* Cooper has encrusted upon it another cumbrous mannerism, that of the periphrasis, not just for the sake of gentility (for this is endemic to all the novels), but for the sake, apparently, of a sort of Ossianic grandeur. It is the device of the riddle or the Old English 'kenning' or of the Authorized Version of some of the Scriptures. The nearest we come to a justification or plausible pretext for this is when Paul Hover in Chapter X exhorts Middleton to tell his story to the ancient Leatherstocking:

'Give it all to the trapper by rule, and by figures of speech,' said Paul, very coolly taking his seat on the other side of the young soldier. 'It is the fashion of old age to relish these ancient traditions . . .'

And it is true that figurative circumlocution nowhere flourishes so rankly as in the mouth of the old man, Natty Bumppo himself:

'. . . Tell me, trapper, where are your Siouxes skulking?'
'It would be as easy to tell you the colours of the hawk that is floating beneath yonder white cloud! When a red-skin strikes his blow, he is not apt to wait until he is paid for the evil deed in lead.'
'Will the beggarly savages believe they have enough, when they find themselves master of all the stock?'
'Natur' is much the same, let it be covered by what skin it may. Do you ever find your longings after riches less when you have made a good crop, than before you were master of a kernel of corn? If you do, you differ from what the experience of a long life tells me is the common cravings of man.'
'Speak plainly, old stranger', said the squatter, striking the butt of his rifle heavily on the earth, his dull capacity finding no pleasure in a discourse that was conducted in so obscure allusions; 'I have asked a simple question, and one I know well that you can answer.' (Chapter VII.)

After page upon page of allusive circumlocutions like these, we certainly echo the squatter's irritation. And yet, dull and torpid as he is said to be, the squatter too cannot explain that the Indians have stolen his cattle, sheep and pigs, as well as his horses, except by saying (Chapter V), 'Then the woman has not a cloven hoof for her dairy, or her loom, and I believe even the grunters, foot sore as they be, are ploughing the prairie.' This must be distinguished from the specially modified Ossianic language which Cooper puts in the mouth of his Indians, for which his precedent must have been the Ossianic prose which Scott fabricates for his Gaelic-speakers, such as Ranald MacEagh in Chapter XXII of *A Legend of Montrose*. In *The Prairie* everyone speaks in this fashion, and one can only suppose that by this means Cooper meant to impart to his narrative some Homeric or otherwise epic dignity and breadth. If so, he fails—and for the usual reason: the action of the story is as implausible as ever, as far from mirroring faithfully the true theme, as far from any internal logic, and in addition is here superfluously complicated (having for instance *two* pairs of lovers to be saved from the Indians by Natty's sagacity).

In fact, the best one can do with Cooper's style in *The Prairie* is to relish the effects of unintended farce which it occasionally provides. The stilted gentility is at its craziest, for instance, in Chapter XI:

'. . . Thy uncle, child'.

'You mean Ishmael Bush, my father's brother's widow's husband,' returned the offended girl, a little proudly.—'Indeed, indeed, it is cruel to reproach me with a tie that chance has formed and which I would rejoice so much to break for ever!'

The humbled Ellen could utter no more, but sinking on a projection of the rock, she began to sob in a manner that rendered their situation doubly critical.

But these hilarious moments are rare.

It is worth labouring this point—that *The Prairie* is so deplorable at the level of language—because it begins and ends with effects of memorable power, and so tends to be remembered as altogether more distinguished than it is. It is astonishing for instance to find Yvor Winters singling it out, along with *The Pioneers*, as the best of the whole Leatherstocking series. One cannot write about Cooper without giving the appearance of special pleading; but to overlook such gross insensitivities as these is to deserve that imputation.

The most illuminating comments on *The Prairie* are those in the *Virgin Land* of Henry Nash Smith. I have in mind not so much the pages he specifically devotes to the Leatherstocking series (pp. 64–76), though these explain the matter of the two pairs of lovers. Much more instructive is the explanation, from the facts of American history (p. 88), of why Cooper had to make Natty, here at the end of his life, a trapper rather than a hunter. And best of all, because partly historical, partly literary, are the pages (pp. 255–260) which explain why the only parts of *The Prairie* which have real distinction—the first and the last chapters—centre upon the figure of Ishmael Bush, the squatter. Professor Smith shows how Cooper's dislike and fear of the settlers of the frontier—the agriculturalists, as opposed to the hunters and trappers *beyond* the frontier—was shared by many conservative Americans of his day, and rationalized by Cooper philosophically in a way which had been formulated many times before, notably by Jefferson:

> The gradations of society, from that state which is called refined to that which approaches as near barbarity as connexion with an intelligent people will readily allow, are to be traced from the bosom of the states, where wealth, luxury and the arts are beginning to seat themselves, to those distant and ever-receding borders which mark the skirts and announce the approach of the nation, as moving mists precede the signs of day.

Thus Jefferson had written, of 'our own semi-barbarous citizens, the pioneers of the advance of civilization'. As Henry Nash Smith puts it succinctly (p. 257):

Although Leatherstocking and Bush figure in the same novel, they belong to entirely distinct conceptual systems. The line that divides them is the agricultural frontier. Leatherstocking, living beyond the frontier and following the vocation of a hunter and trapper, is not a member of society at all. Bush, the husbandman, belongs to society; his 'connexion with an intelligent people' is his participation in the Social compact to which Leatherstocking is not a party.

Bush's indolence and apathy, his brutal power, his sluggish and torpid mind, his physiognomy, his strikingly barbaric taste in dress, the criminality in his past, the biblical and allegorical resonance of his name, Ishmael—all these, as Smith shows, 'are in perfect accord with conservative theory.'

But with Bush in *The Prairie*, as with Leatherstocking himself in *The Pioneers*, Cooper's rational convictions and political allegiances pull one way, even as his imagination tugs him another. In Chapter XI for instance Ishmael and his party make a bivouac:

When each had assumed his proper and customary place around the smoking viands, the squatter set the example by beginning to partake of a delicious venison steak, prepared like the hump of the bison, with a skill that rather increased than concealed its natural properties. A painter would gladly have seized the moment, to transfer the wild and characteristic scene to the canvas.

The reader will remember that the citadel of Ishmael stood insulated, lofty, ragged, and nearly inaccessible. A bright flashing fire that was burning on the centre of its summit, and around which the busy group was clustered, lent it the appearance of some tall Pharos placed in the centre of the deserts, to light such adventurers as wandered through their broad wastes. The flashing flame gleamed from one sun-burnt countenance to another, exhibiting every variety of expression, from the juvenile simplicity of the children, mingled as it was with a shade of the wilderness peculiar to their semi-barbarous lives, to the dull and immovable apathy that dwelt on the features of the squatter, when unexcited. Occasionally a gust of wind would fan the embers; and, as a brighter light shot upwards, the little solitary tent was seen as it were suspended in the gloom of the upper air. All beyond was enveloped, as usual at that hour, in an impenetrable body of darkness.

In a passage such as this Cooper explicitly invites the sort of attention which Henry Nash Smith gives to him, when he goes on:

> Yet the character has an interest for Cooper that defies theory. The idea of Bush's barbarism, along with its connotations of mere criminality, carries a suggestion of moral sublimity. It is related to the moral beauty of Leatherstocking as the somber and tormented landscapes of Salvator Rosa seemed to Cooper and his contemporaries to be related to the mild and smiling landscapes of their other favorite Claude Lorrain.

And Professor Smith is doubtless right to suppose that it was this glimpse of the Salvator-Rosa-picturesque in Ishmael Bush's situation which enable Cooper at the very end of this novel to shoulder clear of his own politics and their philosophical trimmings, free from gentility and the Ossianic, so as to write the sequence in which Ishmael, as a Biblical patriarch, acts according to the ethics of the Old Testament by executing his wife's brother for murder. As Professor Smith notes, the setting for this execution—a night of wind, moonlight and scudding cloud—is meant to recall, and does recall, again a canvas of Salvator Rosa. If anything could have salvaged *The Prairie*, this last surprising and impressive sequence would have done so.

THE PATHFINDER

If it is a matter of rhetoric, properly considered—that is of the management of language—*The Pathfinder* is better than all the other Leatherstocking novels except *The Pioneers*.

It can be called *eloquent*, as for instance *The Deerslayer* cannot.[1]
It is nowhere more eloquent or more moving than in Chapter
VI, where Chingachgook takes a scalp. The last sentences of
Chapter V prepare for the note of unaffected solemnity.
Pathfinder and his young comrade, nicknamed 'Eau-Douce',
are watching from the bank of a river, and recognize Chingach-
gook in the Indian who is swimming towards them:

> '... Now, you see the eye, lad, and it is the eye of a chief. But,
> Eau-Douce, fierce as it is in battle, and glassy as it looks from
> among the leaves',—here the Pathfinder laid his finger lightly
> but impressively on his companion's arm,—'I have seen it shed
> tears like rain. There is a soul and a heart under that red skin,
> rely on it; although they are a soul and a heart with gifts different
> from our own.'
> 'No one who is acquainted with the chief ever doubted that.'
> 'I *know* it', returned the other, proudly, 'for I have consorted
> with him in sorrow and in joy: in one I have found him a man,
> however stricken; in the other, a chief who knows that the women
> of his tribe are the most seemly in light merriment. But, hist!
> It is too much like the people of the settlements to pour soft
> speeches into another's ear; and the Serpent has keen senses. He
> knows I love him, and that I speak well of him behind his back;
> but a Delaware has modesty in his inmost natur', though he will
> brag like a sinner when tied to a stake.'

In Chapter VI, Chingachgook, having reached the bank and
greeted his friends, plunges back into the stream:

> 'What does this mean?—See, the Delaware is swimming to-
> wards the body that is lodged on the rock? Why does he risk
> this?'
> 'For honour, and glory, and renown, as great gentlemen quit
> their quiet homes beyond seas, where, as they tell me, heart has
> nothing left to wish for; that is, such hearts as can be satisfied in
> a clearing, to come hither to live on game and fight the Frenchers.'

[1] This is true at least of the first half of the book; the latter half is a sad
falling-off.

'I understand you—your friend has gone to secure the scalp.'

''Tis his gift, and let him enjoy it. We are white men, and cannot mangle a dead enemy; but it is honour in the eyes of a red-skin to do so. It may seem singular to you, Eau-Douce, but I've known white men of great name and character manifest as remarkable idees consarning their honour, I have.'

'A savage will be a savage, Pathfinder, let him keep what company he may.'

'It is well for us to say so, lad; but, as I tell you, white honour will not always conform to reason, or to the will of God. I have passed days thinking of these matters, out in the silent woods, and I have come to the opinion, boy, that, as Providence rules all things, no gift is bestowed without some wise and reasonable end.'

'The Serpent greatly exposes himself to the enemy, in order to get his scalp! This may lose us the day.'

'Not in his mind, Jasper. That one scalp has more honour in it, according to the Serpent's notions of warfare, than a field covered with slain that kept the hair on their heads. Now, there was the fine young captain of the 60th that threw away his life trying to bring off a three-pounder from among the Frenchers in the last skrimmage we had; he thought he was sarving honour; and I have known a young ensign wrap himself up in his colours, and go to sleep in his blood, fancying that he was lying on something softer even than buffalo-skins!'

'Yes, yes; one can understand the merit of not hauling down an ensign.'

'And these are Chingachgook's colours—he will keep them to show his children's children',—here the Pathfinder interrupted himself, shook his head in melancholy, and slowly added, 'Ah's me! no shoot of the old Mohican stem remains! He has no children to delight with his trophies; no tribe to honour by his deeds; he is a lone man in this world, and yet he stands true to his training and his gifts! There is something honest and respectable in these, you must allow, Jasper.'

And when Chingachgook has got his scalp and given his warwhoop:

Jasper turned away his head as the Delaware rose from the water, in pure disgust at his late errand; but the Pathfinder regarded his friend with the philosophical indifference of one who had made up his mind to be indifferent to things he deemed immaterial. As the Delaware passed deeper into the bushes, with a view to wring his trifling calico dress, and to prepare his rifle for service, he gave one glance of triumph at his companions, and then all emotion connected with the recent exploit seemed to cease.

No less eloquent—in fact, more strikingly so, though not more truly—is Pathfinder's account of the Niagara Falls, in Chapter XIX:

'Well, we went; and though we expected to be led by our ears, and to hear some of that awful roaring that we hear today, we were disappointed, for natur' was not then speaking in thunder as she is this morning. Thus it is, in the forest, Master Cap; there being moments when God seems to be walking abroad in power, and then, again, there is a calm over all, as if his spirit lay in quiet along the 'arth. Well, we came suddenly upon the stream, a short distance above the fall, and a young Delaware, who was in our company, found a bark canoe, and he would push into the current, to reach an island that lies in the very centre of the confusion and strife. We told him of his folly, we did; and we reasoned with him on the wickedness of tempting Providence by seeking danger that led to no ind; but the youth among the Delawares are very much the same as the youth among the soldiers, risky and vain. All we could say did not change his mind, and the lad had his way. To me it seems, Mabel, that whenever a thing is really grand and potent, it has a quiet majesty about it, altogether unlike the frothy and flustering manner of smaller matters, and so it was with them rapids. The canoe was no sooner fairly in them, than down it went, as it might be, as one sails through the air on the 'arth, and no skill of the young Delaware could resist the stream. And yet he struggled manfully for his life, using his paddle to the last, like the deer that is swimming to cast the hounds. At first he shot across the current so swiftly, that we thought he would prevail; but he had miscalculated his distance, and when the truth really struck him, he turned the head up stream, and struggled in a way that was fearful to look at. I could have pitied him, even had he been a Mingo. For a few moments his efforts were so frantic, that he actually prevailed over the power of the cataract; but natur' has its limits, and one faltering stroke of the paddle set him back, and then he lost ground, foot by foot, inch by inch, until he got near the spot where the river looked even and green, and as if it were made of millions of threads of water, all bent over some huge rock, when he shot backwards like an arrow and disappeared, the bow of the canoe tipping just enough to let us see what had become of him. I met a Mohawk, some years later, who had witnessed the whole affair from the bed of the stream below, and he told me that the Delaware continued to paddle in the air, until he was lost in the mists of the falls.'

Here the trivial though natural interest of suspense is entirely dispensed with; we are told that the exploit failed before ever the narration begins. The action is realized as vividly as that in Chapter VII of *The Deerslayer*, more vividly indeed, for the prose here renders the tempo of events. The vividness with which we see the one stroke of the paddle which faltered fatally is at one with the description of the water at the lip of the falls, with its beautifully choice yet inconspicuous epithets, 'even and green'. And yet none of this vividness is there for its own sake, but all to lead up to the clinching image, at once comic and horrific (for only that double aspect truly renders the scale of human against inhuman), of the doomed man still paddling frantically in the air as he falls. The passage is not inferior to Chapter VII of *The Deerslayer*; but it is less important, not central but incidental, it does less work in the narrative as a whole.

It will be noticed that here too the subject is Indian daring and courage. And in fact the best passages of *The Pathfinder* are concerned with the Indians. Thus one suspects that the real motive behind the book was a feeling about Indians. But if so, the plot is once again the wrong vehicle for the vision behind it; and indeed the dissatisfaction one feels with the second half of the story seems to have something to do with the absence of Chingachgook, who figures so largely and memorably in the first hundred pages.

The plot turns instead upon the unsuccessful courtship of Mabel Dunham by Natty, the Pathfinder. This is treated with unexpected delicacy. It has often been remarked that Mabel Dunham is the best of Cooper's heroines, who are for the most part intolerable. If this is true, it has much to do with the fact that Mabel, as a sergeant's daughter, is not quite a lady. And certainly in the same Chapter XIX, where Mabel repels the attentions of the Quartermaster, Cooper brings off what so many of his contemporaries (Scott, for instance, and Charlotte Brontë) tried for repeatedly in vain—a piece of feminine behaviour that is spirited without being pert. Partly because Mabel herself is (though a paragon of virtue) still mildly attractive to the reader, the scene where Pathfinder proposes marriage to her (Chapter XVIII) is truly affecting.

'Affecting', indeed is the word for *The Pathfinder* as a whole; its distinction, where it is distinguished, is the distinction of genuine pathos. Although there is a good deal of blood-letting in the story, the heroic note is quite absent, except for that early episode already quoted, where the pathos of the situation of Chingachgook has a heroic colouring which makes the tone nobly elegiac: 'He has no children to delight with his trophies; no tribe to honour by his deeds; he is a lone man in this world, and yet he stands true to his training and his gifts!'

THE DEERSLAYER

Edmund Wilson[1] endorses the criticism of Cooper by Mark Twain,[2] adding to it a similarly disparaging observation by

---

[1] *The Shock of Recognition*, p. 518.

[2] 'Fenimore Cooper's Literary Offenses', 1895. This justly famous essay is a bitter pill for Cooper's admirers to swallow. But the medicine

Frank Norris;[1] yet he says that both Twain and Norris 'rather miss the point about Cooper'. '*The Deerslayer*', he goes on, 'is not a picture of actual life, but a kind of romantic myth like the stories of Poe, Melville, and Hawthorne . . . The description, at the beginning of *The Deerslayer*, for example, of Glimmerglass Lake, "as limpid as pure air", and of the solitary "castle" in the middle of it owes its power, like Melville's description of the Pacific or one of Poe's pieces on landscape-gardening, to an emotional content which has changed the object and transformed it into a symbol. And the action does have a reality which we recognize and accept as we read: the reality of a dream full of danger.'

This represents what appears to be now the accepted and almost universal attitude taken up towards Cooper by his compatriots; and not towards Cooper only, but (as Wilson implies by the names of Hawthorne and Melville) towards American literature, or at least the American novel, as a whole. None of the American novelists of highest rank—not even James nor Twain himself—is now regarded as belonging to a 'realistic' tradition as that is conceived of in Europe. And there can be no doubt that this change of emphasis is in the main valuable and right.

Yet it has its dangers. Yvor Winters, for instance, from this point of view may seem to be both naïve and as much beside the point as Twain himself when, after allowing that Natty Bumppo is 'a great national myth' (*In Defense of Reason*, p. 186), he nevertheless contends (pp. 190–193) that a reading of Parkman will exculpate Cooper from many of the charges of unreality which Twain brings against him. Yet this is not so; it is quite true that Parkman, a historian unsympathetic to Cooper's portrayal of Indian life, yet himself provides well-

must be taken. It will not do to dismiss it as Marius Bewley does, as 'an unspeakably bad essay' . . . The shrillness there betrays itself; and everything Twain says is true.

[1] From *The Responsibilities of a Novelist*, 1903.

documented evidence of the frontiersman's dexterity in his
appropriate skills, as well as of capacities for devotion, heroism
and moral elevation in the Indians. And there are weightier
reasons why a reader who wants to understand Cooper should
certainly read Parkman before he turns to Hawthorne or Melville or Poe; why indeed Winters is justified in saying that he
who refuses to read Parkman 'is to be commiserated in general
and distrusted in particular as a commentator on certain aspects
of American literature and history.' (p. 191.)

For to read Hawthorne and Poe along with Cooper may
indeed enable the student to see that Cooper's images of
frontier life are not verisimilar transcripts a little shaped and
moulded, but rather symbols and fragments of myth. But what
such reading will not teach is what they are symbols *of*, what
their myth is *about*. And it is a strange though a sadly common
interest in literature which will rest content with discovering
how reality is approached and managed, and never go on to
find out what that reality is. It is all very well to recognize in
The Deerslayer 'the reality of a dream full of danger'; but to
refuse to define what particular dangers are in question is never
to open one's self to the experience of the book at all.

Similarly Winters is more perceptive than Wilson when he
points, for the genuine distinction in the story amid all the
tawdry awkwardness, not to a 'description' but to a situation.
It is true that the descriptions of the Glimmerglass, especially
in the first few pages, embody Wordsworthian perceptions in
Wordsworthian diction, to arresting and convincing effect.
And there are intimations, in all that pertains to the idiot girl
Hetty Hunter, of how Cooper might have harmonized these
perceptions with the characteristically Wordsworthian plot
of *The Idiot Boy* or *The Mad Mother*.[1] As some readers have

[1] The Wordsworthian note in relation to Hetty is nowhere struck more
deeply and truly than in the account (Chapter XXI) of her father's
funeral in the lake: 'To her simple and innocent mind, the remembrance
of her mother brought no other feeling than one of gentle sorrow; a

noticed, Natty Bumppo is not far short of idiocy himself, as when Cooper remarks (Chapter XXII) on 'the childish simplicity so striking, that it frequently appeared to place him nearly on a level with the fatuity of poor Hetty, though always relieved by the beautiful moral truth that shone through all that this unfortunate girl both said and did'. But this is to speak of a novel Cooper might have written, not of the novel that he wrote. For the figure of Hetty is by no means central to the novel as it stands; and in default of a plot centred upon her the descriptions remain incidental. They are often felicitous, and sometimes in ways that go beyond Wordsworth, as in the description of morning twilight in Chapter XIX:

> The day had not yet advanced so far as to bring the sun above the horizon, but the heavens, the atmosphere, and the woods and lake were all seen under that softened light which immediately precedes his appearance, and which, perhaps, is the most witching period of the four-and-twenty hours. It is the moment when everything is distinct, even the atmosphere seeming to possess a liquid lucidity, the hues appearing grey and softened, with the outlines of objects diffused, and the perspective just as moral truths, that are presented in their simplicity without the meretricious aid of ornament or glitter. In a word, it is the moment when the senses seem to recover their powers in the simplest and most accurate forms, like the mind emerging from the obscurity of doubts into the tranquillity and peace of demonstration.

Or, in another, still unWordsworthian way, there is the very accurate and impressive perception of colour at sunset (Chapter XXII):

grief that is so often termed luxurious, even because it associates with itself the images of excellence, and the purity of a better state of existence.'

It would be as faulty to relate this to eighteenth-century sentimentalism in Cooper, as in the case of Wordsworth, for whom 'luxurious grief' is a constant preoccupation.

The logs of the hut and ark had a sort of purple hue, blended with the growing obscurity, and the bark of the hunter's boat was losing its distinctness in colours richer, but more mellowed, than those it showed under a bright sun.

But such felicities are incidental, even though we recognize that the evocation of the wilderness in this way was an essential part of Cooper's undertaking. So it was also for Parkman, who has similar felicities. But of Cooper the novelist we must ask, as of Parkman the historian we may not, that the wilderness be evoked in other ways also, in ways which bear more directly upon action, upon plot. One cannot say of *The Deerslayer* that the wilderness is itself a principal character in the plot, as one can and has to say this of Egdon Heath, in Hardy's *Return of the Native*. (The example is a hackneyed one, but none the less just.)

Winters directs attention to a passage not of description, but of narrative—Chapter VII, where Natty Bumppo kills his first Indian. Here, Winters says, we find 'the instantaneous coincidence of intuition and determinant action'. It is true; and all the intricate moral issues at the heart of the book are here imaged closely in the pause and rush, advance and recoil, of the encounter between the adopted redskin Bumppo fighting the native redskin on behalf of the white man.

It is, however, an incident complete in itself, with only a loose relation to the rest of the plot. And this is to come to the crux of the matter. No one, not Winters nor Wilson nor any other, pretends that the plot of *The Deerslayer* is anything but very bad indeed. But it is not always clear what this means. It does not matter, for instance, that the plot is implausible. Its manifest implausibilities are irritating, chiefly because Cooper himself seems quite unaware of them; but this could be borne with. Similarly one may regret that the plot is not suspenseful; but that too does not in itself condemn it. What is wrong with the plot is that it does not hang together; has no internal logic; one incident does not arise out of another. In short it lacks what

Aristotle called 'unity of action'. And it is this that is disastrous; for it means that the whole train or course of action, instead of being central to the book, the vehicle of its significance, is a mere convenience.

Since writing as above I have looked again at Marius Bewley's revaluation of Cooper in *Scrutiny* (Vol. XIX, No. 2), an essay which I recalled as very fine, and am disconcerted to find that he applauds in *The Deerslayer* just that aspect—of plot as symbolic action—where I most find it wanting. I am tempted to say no more than that I find his account of the book ('the best thing Cooper ever wrote'), as 'incomprehensible' as he finds the judgement of Winters (which I endorse) that it is 'far inferior in plot and movement to half a dozen other stories by Cooper'. But the matter is too important to be left like that. Besides, it would be ungenerous; for I must admit that Mr. Bewley enriches my enjoyment of the book and goes far to vindicate the centrality and symbolic relevance of its plot, when he treats it in terms of a point by point contrast between Leatherstocking's attitude to the wilderness and its inhabitants, and Hurry Harry's. This is just; and I am prepared to agree that when at the very beginning we encounter this couple as 'two men who had lost their way, and were searching in different directions for their path', we are indeed required (though I hadn't seen this for myself) to 'bring a maximum of meaning to this line.' And yet for this opposition to function as a real not a schematic underpinning to this action, Cooper would have to have created Harry as richly and comprehensively, in as much depth, as Leatherstocking, who is opposed to him. I cannot find in Cooper's portrayal of Harry that 'concrete richness', and 'superbly solid physical embodiment' which Mr. Bewley finds. And surely he gives his own game away when he defines the genre of *The Deerslayer* (usefully and rightly) as 'fictional hagiography'. For it is characteristic of hagiography that it cannot give the devil his due; and Cooper gives Harry less than his due, not in the sense that there is anything more to be said for his side of the case, but in the sense that he is, most of the time, a man of straw, two-dimensional, all too rigidly in character whenever he opens his mouth.

And I hold my position the more confidently when I find Mr. Bewley speaking of, not Mabel Dunham, but Judith Hutter, as 'the only real success among his young women', 'the wonderful exception to that great array of female horrors who announce themselves as Cooper's heroines'. For Cooper's portrayal of Judith is not to be judged in terms of literary skill; what is wrong with it is its inhumanity, a cramped littleness, prurience and meanness, the complete lack of magnanimity.

And yet a better case than Mr. Bewley's can be made for the plot of *The Deerslayer*. The clue is in Chapter IX of *The Pathfinder*, where in a eulogistic account of Natty's character we read, 'His feelings appeared to possess the freshness and nature of the forest in which he passed so much of his time; and no casuist could have made clearer decisions in matters relating to right and wrong; . . .'. Cooper's plot, in *The Pathfinder* as in *The Deerslayer*, may be defined as, in no derogatory sense, casuistical. In both novels Natty is placed in a situation where the conflict of loyalties is such as at all points to raise very nice questions of morality. Although the plot of *The Deerslayer* by Aristotelean standards fails so lamentably, yet it is better than the plot of *The Pathfinder*, because Natty's situation in that book—as competing with a younger rival for the hand of a young girl—while it raises nice casuistical questions, does not raise such questions as bear most clearly on his own peculiar status. It is not as a frontiersman, or as the adopted son of an Indian tribe, that Natty has to make choices in his relations with Mabel; but only as a man of a certain age. *The Deerslayer* by contrast has the only plot appropriate to a saint's life; a succession of incidents each providing an opportunity for the saint, by resisting temptations and surmounting obstacles, to prove his saintliness. At this point Cooper is quite out of touch with the novel as conceived of and written by Scott. Marius Bewley once thought Cooper's achievement in *The Deerslayer* was to have rid the plot of the inconsequent picaresque elements still to be found in Scott; so far is this from the case that it would be truer to say that Cooper worked his way (or was pushed by the American reality) out of the world of Scott to a point where a picaresque plot, in the guise of a series of exacting tests, was once again possible and necessary.

IX

THE PIONEERS

D. H. LAWRENCE hardly ever gave a better demonstration of his own sincerity, independence and perceptiveness, than when he praised Cooper wholeheartedly at a time when Cooper was a remarkably unfashionable writer in both England and America:

> I read 'Deerslayer' just before the Turgenev. And I can tell you what a come-down it was, from the pure and exquisite art of Fennimore (*sic*) Cooper—whom we count nobody—to the journalistic bludgeonings of Turgenev. They are all—Turgenev, Tolstoi, Dostoevsky, Maupassant, Flaubert—so very *obvious* and coarse, beside the lovely, mature and sensitive art of Fennimore Cooper or Hardy.[1]

One does not have to concur in the condemnation of the French and Russian writers, in order to be cheered by this rejection of the fashionable in favour of the unfashionable author. Here, as in the *Studies in Classic American Literature*, it is *The Deerslayer* which is singled out for particularly high praise; and this tip has since been taken more than once, and elaborated upon. Yet Lawrence's enthusiasm for *The Pioneers*, the first of the Leatherstocking novels, is almost more interesting. For in

[1] Letter to Catherine Carswell, Nov. 27, 1916. See Harry T. Moore, *The Intelligent Heart*, p. 219; and Armin Arnold, *D. H. Lawrence and America*, pp. 57–58.

The Pioneers, we hardly see the aura of myth which was in the later novels to gather so goldenly about the figure of Leather-stocking. *The Pioneers* is a straightforward realistic novel, immensely rewarding at the level of the literal surface. The image which it presents is rich and dense, not with hidden meanings or allegorical overtones, but simply by virtue of the affectionate exactitude with which Cooper recalls under flimsy fictional disguise his own boyhood in Cooperstown and, in the figure of Marmaduke Temple the patriarchal squire of the new settlement, his own father. Thus we may fairly say that the Lawrence who appreciated *The Pioneers* was the author of *Sons and Lovers* and *The Rainbow*; whereas one feels uncomfortably that the Lawrence who appreciated *The Deerslayer* was a less impressive later Lawrence, the author of allegorical fables like *The Woman Who Rode Away*.

Certainly it is the realism, the vividness of remembered impressions of what was literally there, which Lawrence pays tribute to, in *The Pioneers*:

> There is the actual village itself—the long, raw street of wooden houses, with wood-fires blinking and flashing through the uncurtained windows, in the winter nights. There is the curious, amusing 'Hall' of the village, Judge Temple's somewhat fantastic replica of a squire's residence. The inn, with the drunken Indian; the church, with the snowy congregation crowding to the fire; the astounding Christmas abundance of the tables, that groaned as English tables never groaned, with weight of good things, splendid things to eat; the turkey-shooting, on the snow; the sports of the rough people; then summer coming, with heavy clouds of pigeons, myriads of pigeons, destroyed in heaps; the night-fishing on the teeming, virgin lake; the deer-hunting, the forests all green, the maple-sugar taken from the trees—all this is given with a beauty and a magnificence unsurpassable.[1]

I take this from the earliest version of Lawrence's essay

[1] 'Studies in Classic American Literature (V)' by D. H. Lawrence. *The English Review*, March 1919.

on the Leatherstocking novels, printed in *The English Review*. For as Armin Arnold notices, Lawrence's tone in the revised version which went into hard covers is a good deal less attractive—'derisive, disrespectful, somehow affected'.[1] Judge Temple's 'hall', for instance, which in this first version was 'curious, amusing', becomes in the end 'ridiculous, commodious'. The Lawrence who revised the essays for the book in 1922 or 1923 was already the man who wrote *The Woman Who Rode Away*. In the book we read:

> Perhaps my taste is childish, but these scenes in *Pioneers* seem to me marvellously beautiful. The raw village street, with wood-fires blinking through the unglazed window-chinks, on a winter's night. The inn, with the rough woodsmen and the drunken Indian John; the church, with the snowy congregation crowding to the fire. Then the lavish abundance of Christmas cheer, and turkey-shooting in the snow. Spring coming, forests all green, maple-sugar taken from the trees: and clouds of pigeons flying from the south, myriads of pigeons, shot in heaps; and night-fishing on the teeming, virgin lake; and deer-hunting.
>
> Pictures! Some of the loveliest, most glamorous pictures in all literature.
>
> Alas, without the cruel iron of reality. It is all real enough. Except that one realizes that Fenimore was writing from a safe distance, where he would idealize and have his wish-fulfilment.

The revision deserves study on its own account. (We might well ponder, for instance, 'lavish abundance of Christmas cheer' for 'weight of good things, splendid things to eat; . . .') But there can surely be no doubt, from the new found hesitation at the start ('Perhaps my taste is childish'), and still more from the jaunty sneer which costs so little, 'Fenimore', that the rewriting represents Lawrence going back on his own perceptions, yet without conviction; not a genuine re-thinking but only hedging.

Later writers on *The Pioneers* seem to have agreed that if

[1] Arnold, *op. cit.*, p. 61.

Lawrence did admire these scenes in the book, his taste was indeed 'childish'. At any rate we look in vain among later commentators for the enthusiasm which Lawrence expresses for these episodes. Recent accounts of the book have emphasized other things:

> The emotional and literary center of the story is a conflict between Judge Temple and the old hunter Leatherstocking which symbolizes the issues raised by the advance of agricultural settlement into the wilderness. In the management of this theme Cooper is at his best. From the opening scene, when Judge Temple claims as his own a deer that Leatherstocking's young companion has shot, until the moment when the Judge sentences the old hunter to a fine and imprisonment because of his resistance to the new game laws, the narrative turns constantly about the central issue of the old forest freedom versus the new needs of a community which must establish the sovereignty of law over the individual.[1]

This too appeared in the original essay by Lawrence:

> It is the same bitter tale of the horrid advance of civilisation that subjects all life to its mechanisation of laws and penalties and benevolent Providence. Over the whole world we hear the great wail of natural life under the triumph of civilisation.

This, I suppose is quite touchingly naïve; and Henry Nash Smith does well to analyse 'the horrid advance of civilization' as Cooper deals with it, in terms of the specifically American form that this process took and the debates it had already provoked in Cooper's America, and also by showing Cooper's fertile ambivalence about it—'if the father rules, and rules justly, it is still true that in this remembered world of his childhood Cooper figures as the son. Thus he is able to impart real energy to the statement of the case for defiance and revolt.'[2] Still, the question remains of episodes like the pigeon-

[1] Henry Nash Smith, *Virgin Land. The American West as Symbol and Myth*, pp. 67–68.   [2] *loc. cit.*

shooting, the night-fishing, the making of maple-sugar. Is it true that these, however attractive in themselves, are no more than genre pictures, having no intimate or necessary relation to the main symbolic action? Such adventitious sketchings and documentations occur in Maria Edgeworth's Irish stories, which first provoked Scott into writing, and they recur when Scott in turn serves as model to unskilled writers like the brothers Banim in Ireland; are they to be found in 'the American Scott' also?

They are a perpetual possibility, as a risk or a temptation, in the Scott tradition. And, after all, in the Irish writers too they are often informed with warm affection and humanity. Yet Lawrence himself, at least in the first instance, perceived that these scenes in *The Pioneers* amount to more than this; he realized, as his phrasing makes clear, that through these scenes Cooper was able to convey the impression of natural plenitude. And Nash Smith too, when he says that Cooper's narrative 'turns constantly' about one 'central issue', must mean (if his 'constantly' is to be taken seriously) that he too can see how these passages are knit with the central symbolic action of the story.

They are so knit; and in such a way as to enrich, while complicating, the conflict between Judge Temple and Leather-stocking. By not attending to them directly, Smith's account of the book, like others I have seen, makes it seem to be too much of an open-and-shut case, too predictable, its structure schematic, almost allegorical. And as Lawrence testifies, this is not what it feels like at all, in the experience of reading.

The night-fishing, the pigeon-shoot, the drawing-off of maple-sugar—all these episodes complicate the issue between the Judge and Leatherstocking, because in all these cases the Judge and the hunter stand together, opposed to the mores of their society. Those mores are embodied very powerfully in a figure who is hardly ever mentioned in critical accounts of *The Pioneers*, though he is one of the triumphs of the book.

This is Billy Kirby, Leatherstocking's redoubtable opponent at the Christmas turkey-shoot, expert lumberman and maker of maple-sugar; both in what he stands for, and in the solidity with which he takes his stand as a created character, he is weighty enough to be an effective counterpoise to Leatherstocking and Judge Temple together, on those issues where these two find themselves on the same side of the fence. We meet him first in Chapter XVII, at the shooting of the Christmas turkey:

He was a noisy, boisterous, reckless lad, whose good-natured eye contradicted the bluntness and bullying tenor of his speech. For weeks he would lounge around the taverns of the county, in a state of perfect idleness, or doing small jobs for his liquor and his meals, and cavilling with applicants about the prices of his labour: frequently preferring idleness to an abatement of a tittle of his independence, or a cent in his wages. But when these embarrassing points were satisfactorily arranged, he would shoulder his axe and his rifle, slip his arms through the straps of his pack, and enter the woods with the tread of a Hercules. His first object was to learn his limits, round which he would pace, occasionally freshening, with a blow of his axe, the marks on the boundary trees; and then he would proceed, with an air of great deliberation, to the centre of his premises, and, throwing aside his superfluous garments, measure, with a knowing eye, one or two of the nearest trees that were towering apparently into the very clouds as he gazed upwards. Commonly selecting one of the most noble, for the first trial of his power, he would approach it with a listless air, whistling a low tune; and wielding his axe, with a certain flourish, not unlike the salutes of a fencing master, he would strike a light blow into the bark, and measure his distance. The pause that followed was ominous of the fall of the forest, which had flourished there for centuries. The heavy and brisk blows that he struck were soon succeeded by the thundering report of the tree, as it came, first cracking and threatening, with the separation of its last ligaments, then threshing and tearing with its branches the tops of its surrounding brethren, and finally meeting the ground with a shock but little inferior to an earth-quake. From that moment the sounds of the axe were ceaseless, while the falling of the trees was like a distant cannonading; and the daylight broke into the depths of the woods with the suddenness of a winter morning.

One does not need to have looked forward to *The Prairie*, where a grove of trees has to be conjured up on the treeless prairie so that Ishmael Bush and his family may symbolically fell them, to realize that here too, in *The Pioneers*, the sound of the axe is for Cooper the sound of doom, the sound of spendthrift depredation which will exhaust astoundingly soon the forest plenitude that seems so inexhaustible. It is not for nothing that the trees tower 'apparently into the very clouds', nor that Billy first assails 'one of the most noble'. Billy Kirby carries more weight than Ishmael Bush as Leatherstocking's antagonist (not to speak of that cardboard cut-out of *The Deerslayer*, Hurry Harry), precisely because Cooper allows him good humour and an innate generosity of temper, admires him for his sturdiness and self-sufficiency, and concedes him even a sort of gallantry—he wields his axe 'with a certain flourish, not unlike the salutes of a fencing master . . .' That is to say, Billy is not wholly without a rudimentary poetic sense of the symbolic nature of his own activity, and can honour, in some inarticulate way, the dignity of the forest which is his predestined victim. Yet what comes over, all the better for being accompanied by these more admirable traits of human capacity, is the murderously, irresistibly destructive power that sleeps in his lethargy and casual fecklessness:

For days, weeks, nay months, Billy Kirby would toil, with an ardour that evinced his native spirit, and with an effect that seemed magical, until, his chopping being ended, his stentorian lungs could be heard emitting sounds, as he called to his patient oxen, which rung through the hills like the cries of an alarm. He had been often heard, on a mild summer's evening, a long mile across the vale of Templeton; when the echoes from the mountains would take up his cries, until they died away in feeble sounds from the distant rocks that overhung the lake. His piles, or, to use the language of the country, his logging, ended, with a despatch that could only accompany his dexterity and Herculean strength, the jobber would collect together his implements of labour, like the heaps of timber, and march away, under the blaze of the prostrate forest, like the conqueror of some city, who having first prevailed over his adversary, applies the torch as the finishing blow to his conquest.

It goes without saying that here, as in no other volume of the Leatherstocking series, Cooper's use of language requires no apology; on the contrary one is lost in admiration at the way in which every item tells. When Kirby collects together his tools, 'like the heaps of timber', this signifies that his attitude to the wilderness he despoils is identical with how he sees his 'implements of labour', utilitarian. The trees are indeed implements, things to be used. Again, when his cries to his oxen ring 'like the cries of an alarm', of course that is precisely what they are—an alarm announcing to any who listens 'on a mild summer's evening', that summer has been changed to winter, as the axe has let light into the woods 'with the suddenness of a winter morning'.

As for the fire which Billy Kirby leaves in his wake, 'like the conqueror of some city, who . . . applies the torch as the finishing blow to his conquest', we surely remember it at the end of the book (Chapters XXXVII and XXXVIII) when we read of the vast forest-fire in which the heroine almost perishes. For one character does perish in the fire, and he is a figure far more significant and pathetic than the heroine; it is Indian John, last of the rightful Indian overlords of the whole territory, destroyed by the shame of his own drunkenness more than by the fire, and yet with a profound rightness perishing in the fire which destroys the forest that was his home. Only the later novels of the series will reveal that this degenerate ancient was once the Great Serpent of the Delawares, Chingachgook,

who is to equal in mythical stature the white hunter Leatherstocking himself; yet when he rejects the consolations of the
Christian minister, and among the flames dies erect, his arm
outstretched towards the west, he has already dignity enough
for the symbolic rightness of his end to tell immensely. For the
fire comes about as a direct result of the settlers' improvidence
in ransacking the natural bounty about them:

> The villagers were accustomed to resort to that hill in quest of
> timber and fuel; in procuring which, it was their usage to take
> only the bodies of the trees, leaving the tops and branches to
> decay under the operations of the weather. Much of the hill was,
> consequently, covered with such light fuel, which, having been
> scorching under the sun for the last two months, was ignited with
> a touch. Indeed, in some cases, there did not appear to be any
> contact between the fire and these piles, but the flames seemed to
> dart from heap to heap, as the fabulous fire of the temple is repre-
> sented to relumine its neglected lamp.

In the temple of the forest, the sanctuary lamp has indeed been
neglected, and it shows how it can reassert its own violated
claims. In the words of the youthful and guileless Lawrence,
'Over the whole world we hear the great wail of natural life
under the triumph of civilization. But the violated Spirits of
Place will avenge themselves.'

'The first object of my solicitude', says the Judge in Chapter XX, 'is to protect the sources of this great mine of comfort
and wealth from the extravagance of the people themselves'.
Here the comfort and wealth is that of maple-sugar, and the
mine is the maple-tree. The Judge's concern is shared by no one
but Leatherstocking. The Judge's relative and bailiff, Richard
Jones, and Jones's associate, the English servant Benjamin
Penguilliam, scoff at the Judge's attempts to take precautions.
And so of course does Billy Kirby:

> 'It grieves me to witness the extravagance that pervades this
> country', said the Judge, 'where the settlers trifle with the bless-

ings they might enjoy, with the prodigality of successful adventurers. You are not exempt from the censure yourself, Kirby, for you make dreadful wounds in these trees, where a small incision would effect the same object. I earnestly beg you will remember, that they are the growth of centuries, and when once gone, none living will see their loss remedied.'

'Why, I don't know, Judge', returned the man he addressed: 'It seems to me, if there's a plenty of anything in this mountaynious country, it's the trees. If there's any sin in chopping them, I've a pretty heavy account to settle; for I've chopped over the best half of a thousand acres, with my own hands, counting both Varmount and York states; and I hope to live to finish the whull, before I lay up my axe . . .'

The forest fire at the end of the story shows that the Judge was right. When he acts so as to enforce a close season for game, he is acting in the spirit of the sentiments he expresses among the maple-trees; for the game like the timber must be protected from the thriftless extravagance of the settlers. But he acts through the law, which proves itself an inefficient instrument; for the letter of the law singles out as a culprit the one man who like the Judge, and more than the Judge, acts in the spirit of the law. It is Leatherstocking who is tried and imprisoned for breaking the game laws; and (bitter irony) it is Billy Kirby who is called on by the law to bring Leatherstocking to justice.

For Leatherstocking, even though he does take a deer in the close season, is more consistent even than Marmaduke Temple himself, in abhorring the wanton exploitation of natural resources. This is emphasized in both the lake-fishing and the pigeon-shooting; and it is what lifts both these episodes from the level of genre pictures. The pigeon-shoot, in Chapter XXII, is introduced by a splendid image of two eagles:

For a week, the dark covering of the Otsego was left to the undisturbed possession of two eagles, who alighted on the centre of its field, and sat eyeing their undisputed territory. During the presence of these monarchs of the air, the flocks of migrating birds avoided crossing the plain of ice, by turning into the hills, apparently seeking the protection of the forests, while the white and bald heads of the tenants of the lake were turned upward, with a look of contempt. But the time had come, when even these kings of birds were to be dispossessed. An opening had been gradually increasing, at the lower extremity of the lake, and around the dark spot where the current of the river prevented the formation of ice, during even the coldest weather; and the fresh southerly winds, that now breathed freely upon the valley, made an impression on the waters. Mimic waves began to curl over the margin of the frozen field, which exhibited an outline of crystallisations, that slowly receded towards the north. At each step the power of the winds and the waves increased, until, after a struggle of a few hours, the turbulent little billows succeeded in setting the whole field in motion, when it was driven beyond the reach of the eye, with a rapidity that was as magical as the change produced in the scene by this expulsion of the lingering remnant of winter. Just as the last sheet of agitated ice was disappearing in the distance, the eagles rose, and soared with a wide sweep above the clouds, while the waves tossed their little caps of snow into the air, as if rioting in their release from a thraldom of five months' duration.

So far from being slackly conventional periphrases, 'these monarchs of the air' and 'these kings of birds' are phrases which function as do the word 'noble' and the reference to the trees' towering crests, in the account of Billy Kirby's exploits with the axe. When, on the very next day, the pigeons start coming north, to be subjected by the settlers to indiscriminate and pointless carnage, the image of the eagles serves as a sort of emblem of the hierarchy observed in the bird-kingdom, until disrupted by the human beings who cannot in their own society observe the same discipline and order. (For Billy Kirby, of course, is aggressively his own master, and the emblem also contains in embryo all of the anti-democratic political attitudes which were to bring Cooper the hatred of his countrymen a decade later.)

The carnage reaches its peak when Richard Jones fires a cannon into the pigeons as they continue to fly over:

Some millions of pigeons were supposed to have already passed, that morning, over the valley of Templeton; but nothing like the flock that was now approaching had been seen before. It extended from mountain to mountain in one solid blue mass, and the eye looked in vain, over the southern hills, to find its termination. The front of this living column was distinctly marked by a line but very slightly indented, so regular and even was the flight. Even Marmaduke forgot the morality of Leatherstocking as it approached, and, in common with the rest, brought his musket to a poise.

For Leatherstocking has at this point already made his attitude clear:

'It's better for you, maybe, Billy Kirby', replied the indignant old hunter, 'and all them that don't know how to put a ball down a rifle barrel, or how to bring it up again with a true aim; but it's wicked to be shooting flocks in this wasty manner; and none do it, who know how to knock over a single bird. If a body has a craving for pigeon's flesh, why! it's made the same as all other creaters, for man's eating; but not to kill twenty and eat one. When I want such a thing I go into the woods till I find one to my liking, and then I shoot him off the branches, without touching a feather of another, though there might be a hundred on the same tree. You couldn't do such a thing, Billy Kirby—you couldn't do it, if you tried.'

But the Judge, after the cannon-shot has wreaked its havoc, can only in a revulsion of nausea set the village boys to wringing the necks of the many birds maimed, not killed. And then, 'Judge Temple retired towards his dwelling with that kind of feeling that many a man has experienced before him, who discovers, after the excitement of the moment has passed, that he has purchased pleasure at the price of misery to others.' The Judge similarly implicates himself with what he disapproves of, when in the very next chapter he lends a hand at the seine-fishing of the lake:

'Pull heartily boys', cried Marmaduke, yielding to the excitement of the moment, and laying his hands to the net with no trifling addition to the force.

And yet, in Chapter XIV, when he was asked in the tavern what news he brought 'from the legislature', Temple had approved a law prohibiting precisely this practice:

'The legislature have been passing laws', continued Marmaduke, 'that the country much required. Among others, there is an act prohibiting the drawing of seines, at any other than proper seasons, in certain of our streams and small lakes; and another, to prevent the killing of deer in the teeming months. These are laws that were loudly called for, by judicious men; nor do I despair of getting an act, to make the unlawful felling of timber a criminal offence.'

There in the tavern Leatherstocking had objected to these enactments, not on the score that they were unnecessary or unjust, but because they could not be properly enforced; and he is proved right in the outcome, when he is apprehended under the game laws while both Kirby and Richard Jones the Sheriff (so created at Temple's instigation) are among those who apprehend him. In fact, at the fishing, as immediately before at the pigeon-shoot, Leatherstocking and his Indian associate are alone in endorsing the Judge's attitude, and they go beyond him by acting accordingly:

'No, no, Judge,' returned Natty, his tall figure stalking over the narrow beach, and ascending to the little grassy bottom where the fish were laid in piles: 'I eat of no man's wasty ways. I strike my spear into the eels or the trout, when I crave the creaters; but I wouldn't be helping to such a sinful kind of fishing for the best rifle that was ever brought out from the old countries. If they had fur like a beaver, or you could tan their hides like a buck, something might be said in favour of taking them by the thousands with your nets; but as God made them for man's food, and for no other disarnable reason, I call it sinful and wasty to catch more than can be eat.'

'Your reasoning is mine: for once, old hunter, we agree in opinion; and I heartily wish we could make a convert of the Sheriff. A net of half the size of this would supply the whole village with fish for a week, at one haul.'

But Leatherstocking rejects this alliance with the Judge (for 'you fish and hunt out of rule'); and the Sheriff rejects the very idea 'with great indignation and spleen':

'A very pretty confederacy, indeed! Judge Temple, the land-lord and owner of a township, with Nathaniel Bumppo, a law-less squatter, and professed deer-killer, in order to preserve the game of the county! But, duke, when I fish, I fish; so away, boys, for another haul, and we'll send out wagons and carts in the morning to bring in our prizes.'

This exchange only makes explicit what has been conveyed more memorably, in a sustained and beautifully wrought image, when after the turmoil and turbulence of the drawing of the seine (in which, as at the pigeon-shoot, Billy Kirby is conspicuous), the canoe of Leatherstocking is seen approaching from the opposite shore of the lake:

Through the obscurity, which prevailed most immediately under the eastern mountain, a small and uncertain light was plainly to be seen, though as it was occasionally lost to the eye, it seemed struggling for existence. They observed it to move, and sensibly to lower, as if carried down the descent of the bank to the shore. Here, in a very short time, its flame gradually expanded, and grew brighter, until it became of the size of a man's head, when it continued to shine, a steady ball of fire.

Such an object, lighted as it were by magic, under the brow of the mountain, and in that retired and unfrequented place, gave double interest to the beauty and singularity of its appearance. It did not at all resemble the large and unsteady light of their own fire, being much more clear and bright, and retaining its size and shape with perfect uniformity.

When the light is finally revealed as the lamp of Leatherstocking's canoe, the straightforward observation of literal fact—that it was clearer and brighter than 'the large and unsteady light' of the seine-fishermen's fire—takes on moral reverberations. Yet the literal description is never in danger of thinning out as merely the first level of an allegory; on the contrary, as the light approaches, it is observed ever more intently:

> In addition to the bright and circular flame, was now to be seen a fainter, though a vivid light, of an equal diameter to the other at the upper end; but which, after extending downward for many feet, gradually tapered to a point at its lower extremity. A dark space was plainly visible between the two; and the new illumination was placed beneath the other; the whole forming an appearance not unlike an inverted note of admiration. It was soon evident that the latter was nothing but the reflection, from the water, of the former; and that the object, whatever it might be, was advancing across, or rather over, the lake, for it seemed to be several feet above its surface, in a direct line with themselves . . .
>
> A brilliant, though waving flame, was now plainly visible, gracefully gliding over the lake, and throwing its light on the water in such a manner as to tinge it slightly; though in the air, so strong was the contrast, the darkness seemed to have the distinctness of material substances, as if the fire were imbedded in a setting of ebony. This appearance, however, gradually wore off; and the rays from the torch struck out and enlightened the atmosphere in front of it, leaving the background in a darkness that was more impenetrable than ever.

§2

If due weight is given to the episodes just discussed, it is not possible to define the central issue of the book in the terms of Henry Nash Smith, as 'the old forest freedom versus the new needs of a community which must establish the sovereignty of law over the individual'. When Leatherstocking at the end of the novel sets out for the wilderness he is not rejecting the sovereignty of law but only the practicability of ever enforcing it. Thus the opposition is not between freedom and law, but between freedom and anarchy. For Judge Temple stands for no more than a pious intention, an intention which we are shown clearly can never be fulfilled.

All the same, the contention of Nash Smith that the novel 'turns constantly' about one 'central issue' is thoroughly vindicated. Indeed it can hardly be insisted on too much while it is still possible to say that 'the characteristic adventure of a Cooper novel' is 'not to be confused with the "plot"'; to speak of his 'tiresome, conventional plots'.[1] Henry Nash Smith on *The Pioneers*,[2] and (though less certainly) Marius Bewley on *The Deerslayer*, should have made it impossible to maintain that, 'Looked at squarely, Cooper's novels betray an astonishing lack of co-ordination between the classical ingredients of narrative: plot and character and thought and diction', or that 'his success was marginal precisely in the sense that the most illuminating clashes and insights occur on the margins of his plots'.[3] This is true only if 'plot' is perversely narrowed to mean the love-interest which Cooper thought he had to provide.

In any case it would be wrong to imply that no descriptions or episodes can be tolerated in a novel unless they can be shown, every one of them, to bear directly and immediately on the moral distinction which the novel as a whole seeks to establish. This challenge emerges and has to be met in respect of episodes like the pigeon-shoot, the fishing, and the making of maple-sugar, because these so plainly offer themselves as set-pieces.

[1] R. W. B. Lewis, *The American Adam* (1955), pp. 99, 100.
[2] Nash Smith acknowledges a debt in this matter to Roy Harvey Pearce, whose article in the *South Atlantic Quarterly* (1947) I haven't been able to consult. [3] Lewis, *op. cit.*, p. 101.

But other, more incidental felicities can be justified on other, far simpler grounds:

> The subject of any novel can be told in a few words and in this form holds no interest. A summary narration is not to our taste; we want the novelist to linger and to grant us good long looks at his personages, their being, and their environment, till we have had our fill and feel that they are close friends whom we know thoroughly in all the wealth of their lives. This is what makes of the novel an essentially slow-moving genre, as either Goethe or Novalis observed. I will go even further and say that today the novel is, and must be, a sluggish form—the very opposite therefore of a story, a 'serial', or a thriller.[1]

When we hear that the characters of a novel must become 'close friends whom we know thoroughly', we are nowadays suspicious, and rightly, for this is the principle which has been used repeatedly to make a case for novels which turn out on inspection to have no structure, no relation between plot and theme, or else indeed no theme at all, and hence to issue from no firm moral standpoint. This is not of course the overriding demand to make of a novel, and the failure to see this vitiates Ortega y Gasset's formula, 'The Novel as Provincial Life'. Nevertheless he fails only by taking a partial truth for a whole truth. This demand, too, is a legitimate demand to make of the novel. And I cannot leave *The Pioneers* without pointing out that it meets this demand also. It is, again, Lawrence who shows us where to look, at the Judge's 'amusing' mansion:

> Two small glass chandeliers were suspended at equal distances between the stove and the outer doors, one of which opened at each end of the hall, and gilt lustres were affixed to the frame-work of the numerous side doors that led from the apartment. Some little display in architecture had been made in constructing these frames and casings, which were surmounted with pediments, that bore each a little pedestal in its centre: on these pedestals

---

[1] Ortega y Gasset, 'Notes on the Novel', in *The Dehumanization of Art, and other writings on Art and Culture* (Anchor Books, p. 61).

were small busts in blacked plaster of Paris. The style of the pedestals, as well as the selection of the busts, were all due to the taste of Mr. Jones. On one stood Homer, a most striking likeness, Richard affirmed, 'as any one might see, for it was blind'. Another bore the image of a smooth visaged gentleman, with a pointed beard, whom he called Shakspeare. A third ornament was an urn, which, from its shape, Richard was accustomed to say, intended to represent itself as holding the ashes of Dido. A fourth was certainly old Franklin, in his cap and spectacles. A fifth as surely bore the dignified composure of the face of Washington. A sixth was a nondescript, representing 'a man with a shirt collar open', to use the language of Richard, 'with a laurel on his head —it was Julius Caesar or Dr. Faustus; there were good reasons for believing either'.

The walls were hung with a dark, lead-coloured English paper, that represented Britannia weeping over the tomb of Wolfe. The hero himself stood at a little distance from the mourning goddess, and at the edge of the paper. Each width contained the figure, with the slight exception of one arm of the general, which ran over on the next piece, so that when Richard essayed, with his own hands, to put together this delicate outline, some difficulties occurred that prevented a nice conjunction; and Britannia had reason to lament, in addition to the loss of her favourite's life, numberless cruel amputations of his right arm. (Chapter V.)

The unwonted clarity and vigour of Cooper's prose in this novel is in no other respect so surprising as in his humour; for Cooper's attempts at comic relief are in general monstrously laborious and ineffective. The affectionate and inventive ridicule of this passage strikes unmistakably the note of Dickens, a tone which Lawrence too was capable of, in *The Lost Girl*. And here, as in *The Lost Girl*, it is devoted to a re-creation in depth of the quality of provincial life, its limitations defined at the same time as its humanity is applauded:

To turn each reader into a temporary 'provincial' is the great secret of the novelist. Instead of widening the horizon—what

novelistic horizon could be wider and richer than the humblest
real one?—he must contract and limit it. Thus and only thus can
he make the reader care about what is going on inside the novel.

No horizon . . . is interesting for its content. Any one of them
is interesting through its *form*—its form as a horizon, that is,
as a cosmos or complete world.[1]

It is the sketchiness of Pushkin's gestures in this direction that
makes one suspect that *The Captain's Daughter* is not a true
novel; in Pushkin's hands the form is hardly 'sluggish' enough.
No such suspicions arise in respect of *The Pioneers*.

And yet there is more to it than this. The lavishness of *Pan
Tadeusz*, I have argued, is better than the elegant economy of
The Captain's Daughter because nothing but a leisurely dwelling upon and elaborating of each least item can convey that
Romantic conviction which Scott and Wordsworth share, of
the endlessly ramifying subtlety which weaves together man
with man inside a human society. Where the object is to show
that the weave is frail or frayed or broken, the point can be
made only in the same way—by parting the threads here, and
here, and here. And it is for this reason that *The Pioneers* had
to be dense and close and leisurely. For what Cooper's novel
does, by probing patiently the texture of provincial life in
America, is to establish that this society is not, nor will ever
be, a true community; that it is not a society at all, in any but
a merely formal sense. And the leaving of it, time and again,
for the wilderness—this becomes a duty for all men of integ-
rity and generous feeling.

[1] Ortega y Gasset, *op. cit.*, p. 83.

X

COOPER AND SCOTT:
THE WATER WITCH

卅卅卅卅卅卅卅卅卅 卅卅卅卅卅卅卅卅卅卅卅卅卅卅卅卅卅卅卅卅卅卅卅

SOONER or later, in any attempt to come to terms with
Scott, the question arises whether his 'romanticism' is
real and deep or only a superficial wash of colour laid over
a structure of thought and feeling which is firmly neo-classical.
Patrick Cruttwell has lately decided confidently for the second
alternative, but I think he is mistaken. It is worth while opening
the question afresh, from the point of view of the historio-
grapher, not the literary historian.

Forty years ago, it seemed to G. M. Trevelyan that Scott
was clearly a romantic historian, and in a most valuable way:

> Gibbon was scarcely in his grave when a genius arose in
> Scotland who once and probably for ever transformed mankind's
> conception of itself from the classical to the romantic, from the
> uniform to the variegated. Gibbon's cold, classical light was re-
> placed by the rich mediaeval hues of Walter Scott's stained glass.
> To Scott each age, each profession, each country, each province
> had its own manners, its own dress, its own way of thinking,
> talking and fighting. To Scott a man is not so much a human
> being as a type produced by special environment whether it be
> a border-farmer, a mediaeval abbot, a cavalier, a covenanter, a
> Swiss pikeman, or an Elizabethan statesman. No doubt Scott
> exaggerated his theme as all innovators are wont to do. But he
> did more than any professional historian to make mankind

advance towards a true conception of history, for it was he who
first perceived that the history of mankind is not simple but complex, that history never repeats itself but ever creates new forms
differing according to time and place.[1]

Trevelyan here claims more for Scott than Scott ever claimed
for himself; in *Waverley*, for instance, in his armorial metaphor
about the bearings remaining constant while the tincture
changes, Scott is trying to define some middle position between
the alternatives Trevelyan opposes so categorically, and he
comes down finally on the 'classical' side of the fence.

A famous case, and an instructive one, is Dugald Dalgetty
in *A Legend of Montrose*. When Scott in his introduction
explains the type he has in mind, he seems to do all that Trevelyan claims for him; he particularizes very exactly the condi-
tioning which produced this type at just one period and out
of just one soil:

> The concept of commerce entertained by young men having
> some pretence to gentility, the poverty of the country of Scot-
> land, the national disposition to wandering and to adventure,
> all conduced to lead the Scots abroad into the military service of
> countries which were at war with each other. They were dis-
> tinguished on the Continent by their bravery; but in adopting
> the trade of mercenary soldiers, they necessarily injured their
> national character. The tincture of learning, which most of them
> possessed, degenerated into pedantry; their good breeding be-
> came mere ceremonial; their fear of dishonour no longer kept
> them aloof from that which was really unworthy, but was made
> to depend on certain punctilious observances totally apart from
> that which was in itself deserving of praise.

Such a passage must give us pause when we find Mr. Duncan
Forbes flatly and explicitly contradicting Trevelyan, declaring
that Scott 'is not the link between the Romantic movement and

[1] G. M. Trevelyan, *Clio. A muse, and other Essays* (1913), p. 39.

English historiography. He peopled the past with his contemporaries . . .'; and concluded that ' "Local colour", as used by Romantics like Scott or Southey, was not much more than a game of fancy-dress'. Surely, we feel, this is to go too far; Dalgetty, as we encounter him in the novel itself no less than in the introduction, does not strike us as a portrait of one of Scott's contemporaries.

And yet we do not need Mr. Forbes to remind us that Scott was a pupil of Dugald Stewart, and to that degree a child of the Rationalist enlightenment, in order to feel that as soon as the novel gets under way the particularity of Dalgetty, as the unique product of one historical milieu, is being steadily ironed out. In this respect the novel does not live up to the promise of its introduction. The reviewer in the *Edinburgh Review* (No. 55) put his finger at once on what is happening:

> The general idea of the character is familiar to our comic dramatists after the Restoration—and may be said in some measure to be compounded of Captain Fluellen and Bobadil;— but the ludicrous combination of the *soldado* with the Divinity student of Marischal-College, is entirely original; and the mixture of talent, selfishness, courage, coarseness, and conceit, was never so happily exemplified.

This comment Scott himself quotes with approval; and further acknowledges his indebtedness to Lesmahagow. Dalgetty, then, appears as the type, or rather as a variant on the type, of the *miles gloriosus* from ancient Roman comedy up to Flying-Officer Kite. And Scott goes out of his way to emphasize this by introducing the type in his own day in the figure of Sergeant More M'Alpin, in the fictional introduction to the story proper. Thus he vindicates Mr. Forbes; he has indeed 'peopled the past with his contemporaries'. And if Scott is indeed a link between the Romantic movement and English historiography, the link is not where Trevelyan would place it but rather (as I have argued earlier) in Scott's perception of community as more than the sum of the individuals inside it, and of society therefore as something other than a machine of checks and balances.

Scott elsewhere finds the *miles gloriosus* among his own contemporaries. Captain Mungo MacTurk in *St. Ronan's Well* is another case. And in fact, to prove conclusively that Forbes is by and large right about history and human character in Scott, one cannot do better than go to this one of Scott's novels which is not historical at all. *St. Ronan's Well* stands alone as Scott's attempt at a comedy of manners in contemporary society (more or less contemporary, that is—for the last pages reveal that it is set in the time of the Peninsular War). Scott in his introduction professes a sense of temerity in invading the province particularly of 'the ladies', and distinguishes gracefully among them, 'reckoning from the authoress of *Evelina* to her of *Marriage*', 'the brilliant and talented names of Edgeworth, Austen, Charlotte Smith'. And the unsparing distaste with which Scott portrays the spa as a social milieu relates him at once to Jane Austen's distrust of the gadabout in the complete chapters of her *Sanditon*. In Chapter II Meg Dods is given an important speech in which to rationalize this distaste by implying (quite in Miss Austen's spirit, though not in Miss Edgeworth's) that such a milieu breaks down the hierarchical structure of society. But the principal emphasis does not fall here at all, and Scott's reminding us of 'the ladies' is interesting chiefly for throwing into relief how different his writing is from theirs, how old-fashioned he is by comparison. He is in nothing so old-fashioned as in his lack of interest in the particular and the unique, his preference for the type and for 'character' in the old sense of Overbury and Earle. Those names, in fact, may remind us that if this interest is profoundly unRomantic, indeed anti-Romantic, it is also far older than the Enlightenment.

In Chapter III of *St. Ronan's Well*, where the principal members of Scott's school for scandal are introduced in pungent summary, Scott makes no bones about how he is working in terms of the type. For he introduces each new figure, with rather heavy facetiousness, as 'The Man of Law', 'The Man of Religion', and so on. For the modern reader, of course, the question is what lies behind the facetiousness, what there is delightful and valuable for which the facetiousness must be tolerated.

We can recapture in reading Scott that delight in his imaginative fecundity which so astonished his first readers only if we can induce in ourselves the state of mind, common enough for centuries before his time, to which the elaboration upon a type was a natural and characteristic mode for imagination, for 'invention', to work in. The pleasure aimed at is not that of novelty or vividness, but of recognition; it has to do with the way the writer moves naturally from one feature of the figure to another. Each feature is a stock property of the type, but the achievement is to make us as we read recognize each fresh item as predictable indeed and yet, simply from coming at a new place in the itemizing order and enjoying new relations with other items, each feature surprises—'at once just and surprising'. The aesthetic principle at work is that of consonance, of keeping; the pleasure it affords is that not of discovery but recognition, not wonder but reassurance.

The same holds true of that sort of descriptive writing about which the modern reader of Scott differs most from his predecessors; that is to say, Scott's descriptions not of people but of landscapes and scenery. A good example from *St. Ronan's Well* is the opening paragraph of Chapter XXX:

> It was now far advanced in autumn. The dew lay thick on the long grass, where it was touched by the sun; but where the sward lay in shadow, it was covered with hoar-frost, and crisped under Jekyl's foot, as he returned through the woods of St. Ronan's. The leaves of the ash-trees detached themselves from the branches, and, without an air of wind, fell spontaneously on the path. The mists still lay lazily upon the heights, and the huge old

tower of St. Ronan's was entirely shrouded with vapour, except where a sunbeam, struggling with the mist, penetrated into its wreath so far as to show a projecting turret upon one of the angles of the old fortress, which, long a favourite haunt of the raven, was popularly called the Corbie's Tower. Beneath, the scene was open and lightsome, and the robin redbreast was chirping his best, to atone for the absence of all other choristers. The fine foliage of autumn was seen in many a glade, running up the sides of each little ravine, russet-hued and golden-specked, and tinged frequently with the red hues of the mountain-ash; while here and there a huge old fir, the native growth of the soil, flung his broad shadow over the rest of the trees, and seemed to exult in the permanence of his dusky livery over the more showy but transitory brilliance by which he was surrounded.

This is a set-piece, to be imagined as bearing the title, 'An Autumn Morning'. To suppose that its function is to particularize one specific morning is to miss the point entirely—significantly, the next paragraph begins, 'Such is the scene which, so often described in prose and in poetry . . .' There is one grievous lapse of imagination, 'the robin redbreast was chirping his best'; but otherwise the pleasure aimed at and afforded is precisely that of, for instance, the set 'character' of Mr. Winterblossom as summarized in Chapter III. The items are stock properties of autumn—the heavy dew, the early frost, the mist, the falling leaf, the changing colour of the deciduous trees. Each is predictable; what is unforeseeable, what alone affords a margin for imagination, is the order in which they are presented and the way of getting from one to another.

Perhaps the finest example of Scott's descriptive imagination —at least in *St. Ronan's Well*, though it might be hard to equal elsewhere—is the more than six pages given in Chapter XVI to the portrayal of the Reverend Mr. Cargill. The prose here is reminiscent of the first chapters of *Waverley*, in that these pages too are judicious, weighty, Johnsonian; it should be impossible to read them without marvelling at the fertility of

Scott's invention and realizing, moreover, that this is not to be distinguished from the decency and straightness of his humane feeling. Many who respond in this way may suppose (it is what current habits of thought encourage) that the distinction of this writing is in its individualizing of the character thus presented. But this is wrong; last as well as first the Reverend Mr. Cargill is no more than an instance of the stock type of the unworldly and absent-minded student.

A great deal of Cooper's writing is of this kind, demanding just this sort of radical readjustment on the part of the modern reader. And this is surprising. For of course where Cooper is concerned there is no room for argument about whether history ever throws up wholly unprecedented kinds of personality. Cooper presents not just Leatherstocking but Ishmael Bush and others as examples of just such unprecedented characters produced by the pressure of unprecedented historical conditions. Cooper's America, where 'The New Adam' was a rallying cry, had a great deal invested in the conviction that this was indeed possible. Yet Cooper was oddly and consistently out of sympathy with the expansiveness, the hopeful egalitarian ebullience, of those elements in his America which looked for the new Adam most confidently. Himself a stiff-necked melancholy conservative in politics, he seems to have been pushed against his will, almost resentfully, into creating, in Leatherstocking, the most powerful and haunting of all the images of the new Adam. As we have seen, in every one of the Leatherstocking novels there is at least one important type-figure or 'humour' like Dugald Dalgetty. In *The Pioneers* it is Benjamin Penguilliam; and this is from one point of view the best of them (as Dr. Obed in *The Prairie* is certainly the worst), because Penguilliam is an Englishman among Americans, and the settledness of his character, its definite outlines and predictable postures, may be taken to stand for a structure of personality proper to the Old World, among the more fluid and amorphous New World characters around him.

At any rate, there are, even in the Leatherstocking novels, characters which are types or humours like Peregrine Touchwood in *St. Ronan's Well*. And in some of Cooper's other novels this is the only sort of character there is. They are none the worse for this. I am eager to endorse, for instance, Yvor Winters's and Marius Bewley's commendations of *The Water Witch*, a novel conducted entirely within this convention, and heightening the convention, in fact, to a pitch of unreality which Scott never permitted himself. *The Water Witch* is set supposedly in the early days of the colony of New Amsterdam, but there is no pretence that it conveys the feel of what life was like in that place at that time. And this self-confessed unreality comes about, above all, from the techniques of characterization. Alderman Van Beverout, for example, is far more insistently and impossibly 'the man of trade' than Scott's 'man of law' is a man of law. Peregrine Touchwood is always and everywhere the type of the best kind of Whig; yet we are not made to feel that in no conceivable circumstances, at no conceivable time, could he act or speak anything but Whiggery. But with Van Beverout we feel this; he could never act or speak as anything but the merchant. So far from being a Dutch merchant in America in the eighteenth century, he is the type of the mercantile attitude to life, its essence embodied. Because of this resolute and extreme abstraction in the characterization, whenever the Alderman opens his mouth, he can ring the changes upon one entirely predictable and rigid range of references. This constitutes an exacting challenge to Cooper's copiousness of invention; and he rises to the challenge superbly, for ever discovering new images to fit into intricate patterns of syntax and cadence.

Winters remarks[1], 'To the reader who does not find a certain pleasure in the texture of the prose in which the meditations of the Alderman are couched, the Alderman must needs be very tiresome; but his reveries and his commercial imagery possess

[1] Yvor Winters, *In Defense of Reason*, p. 197.

a hard and clear, if somewhat baroque and elaborate, beauty . . .'
Beauty, in fact, there is—of the sort which Winters calls elsewhere 'something approaching pure rhetoric'. And yet the
beauty is not after all there for its own sake. If there is beauty,
there is also *interest*, there is in fact characterization; and if the
characterization is that of Jonson, it is also that of Scott, a
characterization which does not penetrate steadily deeper, nor
does it individualize. Van Beverout is a 'humour', as are all the
other figures in *The Water Witch*, even to such a marginal
actor as Master Trysail, the English sailing-master:

'Though a poor man's son, Captain Ludlow, I am a free-born
Briton, and my education has not been entirely overlooked. I
hope I know something of the constitution, as well as my betters.
Justice and honor being an Englishman's mottoes, we must look
manfully to the main chance. We are none of your flighty talkers,
but a reasoning people, and there is no want of deep thinkers on
the little island; and therefore, sir, taking all together, why,
England must stick up for her rights! Here is your Dutchman,
for instance, a ravenous cormorant; a fellow with a throat wide
enough to swallow all the gold of the Great Mogul, if he could
get at it; and yet a vagabond who has not even a fair footing on
the earth, if the truth must be spoken. Well, sir, shall England
give up her rights to a nation of such blackguards? No, sir;
our venerable constitution and mother Church itself forbid, and
therefore, I say, dam'me, lay them aboard, if they refuse us any
of our natural rights, or show a wish to bring us down to their
own dirty level!'

'Reasoned like a countryman of Newton, and with an eloquence
that would do credit to Cicero! I shall endeavour to digest your
ideas at my leisure, since they are much too solid food to be
disposed of in a minute . . .'

Certainly this is nearer to the accent of imaginable speech, as
it is further from beautiful artifice, than anything Van Beverout
says; just as Trysail has more than one side to him, since we
are allowed to see him in action as an able and gallant seaman.

Nevertheless, this is so invariably his idiom, and these are so
invariably his sentiments, that he is more than a type—he is a
humour. And as with Van Beverout, as with the characters of
Scott, so with Trysail the pleasure we take in him, on his every
appearance after the first, is a pleasure not of discovery but of
recognition; and we admire his creator for fertility of invention
and variation within a rigid frame. There is this much to be said
for Winters's 'pure rhetoric': that the pleasure we take in such
creations is more clearly an aesthetic pleasure than what we
derive from the characters of a Lawrence, a Stendhal or a
Dostoievsky. Yet the achievement is not purely aesthetic in
any limiting way; we can hardly deny to Cooper a moral
achievement when he can permit such mordant and justified
sarcasm ('Reasoned like a countryman of Newton') against
a character who is none the less seen with sympathy and even
admiration.

All the same, the great difficulty remains a comically simple
one: what is *The Water Witch* about? This question arises for
us, so used as we are to realistic conventions, whenever a novelist is plainly not proposing to present human beings in anything approaching the uniqueness which we have to believe is
the condition of human being. If *A Legend of Montrose* is
about the *miles gloriosus*, not about a human being conditioned
to uniqueness by his age and setting, if therefore it is not in any
significant way about Scotland in the seventeenth century,
then what is it about? Where is the point at which the story
breaks through, from antiquarian documentation on the one
hand, and on the other from a thicket of literary conventions
and conventional types (Fluellen, Falstaff, Bobadil, Lesmahagow), to make contact with the life we know? In the case of
A Legend of Montrose, the answer is not hard to find. The
Edinburgh Reviewer thought that Dalgetty showed Scott at
his most Shakespearean, and the critic specially mentioned the
name of Falstaff. The relationship is there, obscured only a
little by Dalgetty's physical bravery. Dalgetty wanders round

the battlefield, a personification of earthy grossness, throwing into highlight the chivalric 'honour' of Lord Menteith, the barbaric 'honour' of Ranald MacEagh, and the feudal 'honour' of the clansmen; his mere presence punctures these pretensions, as Falstaff punctures the pretensions of Hotspur, and yet he stands judged, as Falstaff does, by that very standard which he reveals as absurd. In the novel, too, as in Shakespeare's play, the hero (Montrose or Prince Hal) is the idealist of 'honour' who is able to compromise, play the machiavel, and use the materialists such as Falstaff and Dalgetty. In this way Dalgetty plays Sancho Panza to the various Quixotes who surround him. And Orwell, in his essay 'The Art of Donald McGill' (about comic postcards), is surely right to insist that Sancho Panza isn't a type like the boastful soldier or the absent-minded scholar. At least he is this no longer as soon as Quixote comes to stand beside him. For these two figures, Quixote and Panza (or MacEagh and Dalgetty, or Hotspur and Falstaff), once they are put into mutual relation, express all the ironies and comedies and sorrows of the tension in every man between idealism and self-preservation. *A Legend of Montrose* is thus one of those works which William Empson has called, more wittily than helpfully, and yet quite justly, 'versions of pastoral'.

The problem of *The Water Witch* is not to be solved at all so easily. And yet *A Legend of Montrose* at least tells us where to look for the answer. Indeed, a name such as Jonson has prepared us already. We can expect to find the meaning of the total structure of the novel conveyed in ways that we associate with poetry. And this too can be paralleled in Scott. The best example is *The Bride of Lammermoor*.

At first sight the plot of *The Bride of Lammermoor* is constructed on the same model as *Waverley*, as a confrontation of old and new at a turning-point in history, the confrontation to be resolved, if at all, by marriage. It is thus that David Daiches sees the book:

The Bride of Lammermoor ... presents the conflict of the old
and the new in naked, almost melodramatic terms: the decayed
representative of an ancient family comes face to face with the
modern purchaser of his estates. The book is stark tragedy, for
the attempted compromise—marriage between the old family
and the new—is too much for circumstances, and the final death
of hero and heroine emphasizes that no such direct solution of
the problem is possible.[1]

But this is true, only if it is acknowledged that the circumstances which defeat the attempted compromise consist in
two personalities, and those not the two principals. Circumstances in the sense of historical events and tendencies in fact
favour the reconciliation between the Tory Master of Ravenswood and 'the new man', Sir William Ashton. What defeats
the union is the inflexibility of Lady Ashton combined with,
what is in fact its consequence, the excessive pliability of her
daughter. To be sure, Lady Ashton's rigidity is made historically plausible in that she is a woman of the old order married
to a man of the new, and is therefore particularly sensitive about
status. But Scott goes out of his way to emphasize that this
does not by any means explain, though it may have aggravated,
her fatal hauteur. Scott has gone out of his way—quite against
his normal practice—to show fate working outside, or at any
rate distinct from the historical process. And it is this that justified Edwin Muir in describing *The Bride of Lammermoor* as
'the story in which we have the strongest impression of fate.'[2]

On the other hand Muir is anything but helpful when he
finds 'the secret' of Scott in his unconsummated youthful
passion for Williamina Stuart-Belsches, and declares:

Among the novels, there is most of his secret world in *The
Bride of Lammermoor*, which he wrote in a delirium of pain, so

[1] David Daiches, *Literary Essays*. Mr. Daiches himself seems dissatisfied with this analysis for he argues that Scott is ironical about the
Master of Ravenswood and his servant. This irony I cannot detect.

[2] Edwin Muir, *Essays in Literature and Society* (1944), p. 76.

that he could not remember a single scene when it was shown to him, and found the whole 'monstrous, gross and grotesque'.

That *The Bride of Lammermoor* is a special case, all might agree. But Muir wants his 'secret' to underlie Scott's work as a whole, and does not mind if damaging admissions have to be made in order to get it there:

> The bustle, the energy, the humour and pathos of life are there as they are nowhere else, even in Balzac and Tolstoy; but there is no serious criticism of life. When Scott expresses a judgment of experience it comes from the secret world where the memory of Williamina was buried, and its burden is that all is vanity, the bustle, the adventure, the glory, everything that he created with such genial warmth and abundance:

> > Look not thou on beauty's charming,
> > Sit thou still when Kings are arming . . .
> > Stop thine ear against the singer,
> > From the red gold keep thy finger—
> > Vacant heart, and hand, and eye,
> > Easy live and quiet die.

These admirable verses come in fact from *The Bride of Lammermoor*. They are sung by the doomed bride herself, Lucy Ashton—but long before her doom is upon her or is seen to be inevitable. In other words, the song is in character, and should surely be taken so unless we are given explicit warrant for taking it otherwise. I perceive no warrant for Muir to excerpt it and present it as spoken or sung by Scott *in propria persona*. To take it so is to damage the novel irreparably. For the whole action of the story reveals the impracticability of Lucy's prescription, and appears designed to do just that. The calamitous outcome of the action is in great part the result of Lucy's trying to maintain this neutral attitude; easy life and quiet death are both denied her because of it, because she set them up as her objectives. And here, surely, is precisely that 'serious criticism of life' which Muir denies to Scott with the air of denying him very little. The confrontation of old and new is, then, the basic structure of *The Bride of Lammermoor*, as of *Waverley*—but with this difference: that the confrontation takes place within a single personality, and can never be resolved because the personality refuses to acknowledge its existence.

It is surely fair to describe such a structure for a novel, pivoting on a scrap of verse unobtrusively introduced at a point of no special salience, as *poetic*. It is only an extension of Scott's experiments with epigraphs, which are frequently verse of Scott's own composition. This is something far more subtle than the neat aptness by which, for instance, Chapter XXII of *A Legend of Montrose*, which is to deal with the Highland barbarians the MacEaghs, is made to bear as epigraph the famous lines from *The Conquest of Granada*:

'I am as free as nature first made man
Ere the base laws of servitude began,
When wild in woods the noble savage ran.'

And it is by just so much more impressive, because more inward, less detachable, than the virtuoso brilliance by which Pushkin in *The Captain's Daughter* used the epigraph as a signal in code.

Cooper had given some thought to the use of the epigraph. For when he reviewed Lockhart's *Life of Scott* he objected to Scott's being credited with too much in this respect, as if no one had used epigraphs before him. In *The Water Witch*, in the epigraphs and elsewhere, Cooper quotes from Shakespeare very freely, and Winters remarks sensibly, 'The numerous quotations from Shakespeare employed in this work give a clue to the Elizabethan models for the prose; . . .' It may be that they give a clue to more than that. With *The Bride of Lammermoor* in mind, one wonders if they do not give a clue also about the plot. Winters says of *The Water Witch*:

It has the plot, entrances, exits, abductions, and mysteries of a comic opera; and the style is adjusted to the plot in a manner at once brilliant and meticulous. Plot and character alike have the unreality, but the consistency within themselves, of the plot and character, let us say, of *Volpone*; . . .

But if the conventions which govern the action of *The Water Witch* are the conventions of comic opera, they are equally the conventions of Shakespearean comedy. And this is important; for it affords one way of turning the otherwise unanswerable question, 'What is the novel about?' Winters says of the speeches of Van Beverout and the others:

> The essential difficulty in connection with these rhetorical excursions resides simply in the fact that the subject is never adequate to permit the extraction from the rhetoric of its possibilities, so that we have a species of lyricism, which, though real enough, is frequently all but verbal or even syntactical; we have something approaching pure rhetoric.

On this showing, the theme of the book—if we take 'theme' to be what the overt and preposterous subject or plot merely shadows forth—is very fugitive and elusive. So it is; yet it is no harder to find, and the risk is no greater of breaking a butterfly on a wheel, than in a Shakespearean comedy such as *Twelfth Night*. What emerges, as much from the landscape and seascape-painting as from the intricately patterned speeches of the characters, is a sort of wistful image of what America could have been had she not been from the first under the influence of Northern European bourgeois protestantism. 'The Water Witch' herself, a smuggler's brigantine, her master and her company also, even the luxury articles of lace and brocade which are her stock in trade—these represent, in no allegorical fashion but in terms of timbre and associative resonance, the claims of the mediterranean, above all the Italian way of life, at once mercantile and frankly voluptuous.

From this point of view the imaginative centre of the book is an otherwise unmotivated comparison of the coast and coastal waters of New York with the bay of Naples. The comparison

is invited by the Olivia of the story (significantly perhaps a
Huguenot colonial heiress), and is supplied by the Viola,
the smuggler's consort who masquerades as a man, indeed as
the redoubtable smuggling captain himself. (When she is un-
masked, proving inadequate to masculine action in an emergency,
she is Viola trapped into her duel with Aguecheek.) The comparison, in the form of a vast panoramic word-painting of the
bay of Naples, surges bemused through thousands of words
and over page upon page. By way of 'the graceful and winding
Baian harbour' and 'the ancient Lucrine lake', 'the grotto of
the Sybil' and 'the Cumaean passage', by Pozzuoli and 'noisy
Napoli itself' and the 'vast plain to the right' which held 'the
enervating Capua, and so many other cities, on its bosom',
the incredible mariner is allowed to expatiate on the vista
which was in fact available to Cooper where he sat writing the
book in Sorrento. And it is possible to take this as a particularly
impudent example of the licence which Lever and other harassed
writers of serials quite often allowed themselves, tumbling into
the currently allotted number of pages whatever material was
near at hand. On the other hand this passage is only the con-
centrated statement of an Italianate enthusiasm which crops
out almost comically in quite other parts of the book, whenever an association can be fetched from however far, in order
to justify it. Nothing more than 'velvet', for instance, is required to provoke a brief but sonorous rhetorical excursion
on Venice:

> The lagunes are filling with fat soil, and the keel of the trader
> is less frequent there than of old. Ages hence the plough may
> trace furrows where the Bucentaur has floated! The outer India
> passage has changed the current of prosperity, which ever rushes
> in the widest and newest track. Nations might learn a moral by
> studying the sleepy canals and instructive magnificence of that
> fallen town; but pride fattens on its own lazy recollections to the
> last!

The progression here from 'fat' to 'fattens' is certainly poetic, and this exertion of imagination at the level of words, of the patterns they make and the shocks and collisions between them, is so constant in *The Water Witch* that it is truer, as well as more generous, to put Cooper's sense of Italy at the centre of his book. And the novel then becomes wonderfully all of a piece, the form (the Italianate form of Shakespearean comedy) wonderfully fitted to the matter it expresses. Winters decides, and one is prepared to concur, that 'questions of scope aside, it is probably Cooper's ablest piece of work, as it is certainly one of the most brilliant, if scarcely one of the most profound, masterpieces of American prose.'

Scott never attempted anything in its very conception so brilliant, so original, so eccentric. Yet it would be wrong to say that his imagination never worked along these lines at all. On the contrary, my aim has been to show that the novel as Scott practised the form kept open invaluable avenues of connection with literary forms, and modes of imaginative apprehension, much older, more flexible and more various than we normally think of as within the novel's range. For a last example of how Scott can be 'poetic', I return briefly to *St. Ronan's Well*.

Although in his characterization by way of 'humours' Scott reaches back far farther than to the eighteenth century, yet in *St. Ronan's Well* Scott's prose, though of course much slacker than the prose of Johnson or Jane Austen, still has the judicious weight and sometimes the acerbity of these writers in an eighteenth-century tradition. And it is in the context of these Johnsonian or at any rate Austenesque cadences that Chapter XX, 'Theatricals', comes as such a surprise. It shows how Scott is free of a dimension of the imagination outside Jane Austen's range. The presentation of *tableaux vivants* in the gardens of Shaws Castle is something we are plainly invited, thoroughly in Jane Austen's fashion (though more coarsely), to regard as pretentious tomfoolery; and accordingly we are made to note everything that is ludicrous, mean and undignified about this occasion. Yet Scott's imagination is stirred, as Jane Austen's would not have been, by the Shakespearean charm and decorum aimed at however clumsily, and achieved however fleetingly, by people whom Scott continues to dislike and despise. The lyrical feeling accumulates unobtrusively under the surface of satirical burlesque, and comes to overt though still diffident expression in the last paragraph of the chapter:

Others strolled through the grounds, meeting some quaint disguise at the end of every verdant alley, and communicating to others the surprise and amusement which they themselves were receiving. The scene, from the variety of dresses, the freedom which it gave to the display of humour amongst such as possessed any, and the general disposition to give and receive pleasure, rendered the little masquerade more entertaining than others of the kind for which more ample and magnificent preparations have been made. There was also a singular and pleasing contrast between the fantastic figures who wandered through the gardens and the quiet scene itself, to which the old clipt hedges, the formal distribution of the ground, and the antiquated appearance of one or two fountains and artificial cascades, in which the naiads had been for the nonce compelled to resume their ancient frolics, gave an appearance of unusual simplicity and seclusion, and which seemed rather to belong to the last than to the present generation.

The effect is not that the writer does not know his own mind, nor that the reader does not know which way to take this scene. On the contrary the effect is, all over again, 'at once just and surprising'; and the shift of tone, far from disconcerting, persuades us of a human 'breadth' such as, among Scott's English contemporaries, only Byron in *Don Juan* could sometimes attain. It is common however to the Slavs who learned from both Scott and Byron; and it is, as Marvin Mudrick has pointed out, in particular the great distinction of Mickiewicz.

INDEX